# on track ...
# Joe Jackson

every album, every song

Richard James

sonicbondpublishing.com

Sonicbond Publishing Limited
www.sonicbondpublishing.co.uk
Email: info@sonicbondpublishing.co.uk

First Published in the United Kingdom 2022
First Published in the United States 2022

British Library Cataloguing in Publication Data:
A Catalogue record for this book is available from the British Library

Typeset in ITC Garamond & ITC Avant Garde
Printed and bound in England

Graphic design and typesetting: Full Moon Media

# on track ...
# Joe Jackson

every album, every song

Richard James

sonicbondpublishing.com

## Acknowlegements
To Alison, with the 'smile like a diamond'

I am indebted to Andreas Wostrack of the Joe Jackson Archive Website for his proofreading, comments, and suggestions which have turned this book into something far better than my first draft!

# on track ...

# Joe Jackson

## Contents

# Introduction

Born on 11 August 1954 in Burton-on-Trent, Staffordshire, David Ian Jackson spent the first year of his life in Swadlincote, Derbyshire. The family moved back to Portsmouth, his mother's hometown, and in a council flat in Paulsgrove, the family line-up expanded over time to include two younger brothers. Growing up in working-class poverty led to Jackson becoming a chronic asthmatic, and a sensitive disposition didn't help the young boy during his school days. A lover of books, Jackson was bullied but was not given to violent revenge. Prevented from playing sports due to his medical condition, he turned to books; his original desire of becoming a professional writer was soon overtaken by music. He began playing the violin and joined a class at school, primarily to avoid the bullies. Further stints on the oboe and timpani added to his musical knowledge. A couple of years later he switched to the piano, feeling that this was the instrument which could be the springboard to his new ambition: composer. Instrumental composition and songwriting consumed him, and by the time he was sixteen, he was being paid to play gigs in local pubs.

The eighteen-year-old Jackson passed an advanced 'S' level examination in music that earned him a grant to study at the Royal Academy of Music in London. In the ensuing three years, he worked with a fringe theatre group, studied jazz with John Dankworth, was a member of the National Youth Jazz Orchestra, and played in several pop 'covers' bands. One of these was Edward Bear, where his supposed likeness to the 1960s children's television puppet character 'Joe 90' led to the nickname 'Joe' which stuck and became his public persona.

By the time he left the Royal Academy (with a degree in percussion), he was a songwriter with the group Edward Bear, who were gaining some minor record company interest. Unfortunately, there was another Edward Bear, a Canadian band, (it's the old story, you wait all this time, etc, etc,) who already had a record deal and so Edward Bear turned first into Edwin Bear, finally getting a record deal as Arms And Legs. Two singles were released on MAM Records. The label seemed to have very little interest in the band they had signed, and Jackson left in October 1976.

Jackson's next musical diversion was into cabaret, acting as pianist and musical director for the Portsmouth Playboy Club, saving his earnings to finance the recording of his own album. He left the Playboy Club to tour with the singing duo Koffee n' Kreme between August 1977 and Spring 1978, who came to brief national recognition as a result of appearing on the amateur talent television show New Faces. Income from these activities was also put towards the cost of recording demos of his own songs.

1978 saw Jackson living in London, armed with a fully-fledged album-length demo. He had the talent and determination, the songs, and a band. The demo was turned down by both Stiff and Chiswick Records, and even Virgin Records expressed a lack of interest. Eventually, the tape attracted the attention of David Kershenbaum who was in London scouting for new talent for A&M Records.

Jackson was immediately signed, and the 'album demo' was re-recorded in just two weeks, and issued as 'Look Sharp!' in January 1979.

Fast forward (ahem) 40 years and Jackson has consistently recorded and toured. He has published a memoir (*A Cure for Gravity*), and made numerous guest appearances on other artists' records, including – erm – William Shatner. He has appeared in the film *The Greatest Game Ever Played* as a pub pianist, which also featured some of his music, and worked extensively on a proposed musical *Stoker*, about the creator of Count Dracula. He has been awarded a Fellowship of the Royal Academy of Music, and an Honorary Doctorate by the University of Portsmouth.

A quote from *A Cure for Gravity* succinctly sums Jackson up;

What would I have done if I hadn't been a musician? I haven't a clue. Sometimes I see myself in the sad bastards who mill around outside pubs at closing time, looking for a fight. Sometimes I think that music saved my life.

Not all of Jackson's music is to everyone's taste, obviously. However, every single version of his output shows him to be a consummate musician, an outstanding songwriter, a gifted composer, and a charismatic performer.

# Look Sharp!

Personnel:
Joe Jackson: vocals, piano, harmonica
Gary Sanford: guitar
Graham Maby: bass
Dave Houghton: drums
Recorded at Eden Studio, London, W14
Produced by David Kershenbaum
Engineer: 'Hot' Rod Hewison
Assistant Engineer: Aldo Bocca
All songs written and arranged by Joe Jackson
Released: January 1979 on A&M Records
Highest chart positions UK: 40, USA: 20

Recorded in August 1978, and released six months later, Jackson's debut album sought to capture a spontaneous sound. Reminiscing about the album on his website Jackson concluded:

> What can anyone say about something they did so long ago?! I'm not embarrassed by it, or not by most of it, anyway. It positively reeks of London 1978-79 and, well, it is what it is. I'm glad people liked it, and still like it, though I think some of that is nostalgia and a tendency to romanticise peoples' first albums, as though later ones must somehow be less 'authentic'. For a first album, this one's not bad, but I was only 23 when I made it and it would be pretty weird if I didn't think I'd done better things since.

The album could easily have been called 'Sound Sharp!' The songs breathe energy, attitude, melody, and a recording style which leaves plenty of space for the music to breathe. Despite his eclectic musical background and academic instruction, Jackson was, at this stage, clearly impressed with the 'new wave' movement of the time; his songs echo the energy and simplicity of the style, allied to the outspoken tone of the lyrics. Jackson was adept at incorporating these influences and, if he was sailing under the flag of 'new wave', it was a style which was a good fit for the time.

What reviewers at the time mistakenly took for pseudo-punk disgust was Jackson's tongue-in-cheek attitude; he had served his time in a variety of musical ventures in show business, and his sardonic, intelligent, lyrical commentary supported by razor sharp songs, arrangements and performances served up an intoxicating blend of talent, attitude, and potential.

*Look Sharp!* was re-released in 2001 with two bonus tracks; 'Don't Ask Me' and 'You Got the Fever' which were the B-sides of the single releases of 'One More Time' and 'Is She Really Going Out With Him?' respectively.

## 'One More Time' (3.15)
In *A Cure for Gravity* Jackson recalled;

> I [...] worked on a song called 'One More Time', with a driving guitar riff and
> anguished lyrics about the end of a relationship. The guy can't believe the
> girl wants to leave: tell me one more time, he says, one more time, one more
> time. I'd taken a little piece of my breakup with Jill, one moment, one feeling,
> and embellished it into something else. I guess that's how fiction works: not
> creating something false but creating new truths out of bits of old ones. Just as
> we create new music by endlessly reshuffling the same old chords and scales.

What sounds like it should be a typical 'band encore' song judging by the title
is anything but. The first track of this punchy debut is an unconventional 'end
of relationship' song where the arrangement of the guitar, bass, and drum
playing adds much to the relatively sparse, highly energetic musical texture.

Opening with an aggressive guitar sequence (which will underscore the
chorus) together with a driving high bass line and syncopated drums, Jackson
immediately lays the emotional landscape wide open; 'Tell me one more time
as I hold your hand that you don't love me, Tell me one more time as teardrops
start to fall. Shout it to me and I'll shout it to the skies above me, that there was
nothing after all'. Uncredited backing vocals (which must be a combination of
Sanford, Maby, and Houghton) raise the energy level for the pre-chorus which
builds into a full-on chorus with Maby's high register semi-quaver based bass
line prominent.

The second verse emphasises the narrator's vulnerability; 'Tell me one more
time we never had a thing in common. Tell me one more time as you turn and
face the wall. Tell me I should know you never were my kind of woman. And
tell me we were fools to fall'.

Where the listener may reasonably expect an instrumental section the third
verse appears instead with staccato, syncopated chords for the first two lines;
'Tell me one more time your tears were only sad confusion, and tell me it's just
been so long and that is all'. Full throttle is applied for the remainder of the
verse.

The final chorus is repeated, with the second play-through building on the
energy level. Maby wears his fingers out, and Houghton hits his drums very
hard indeed as this fine opener comes to an abrupt end. The only real criticism
of the song is that the tempo feels too controlled, and when performed in
a live setting the full raw energy of the composition and the band would be
unleashed to better effect.

## 'Sunday Papers' (4.20)
Set against a cheery reggae backing, Jackson's scathing commentary on the
tabloid press of the late 1970s is equally relevant decades later, where 'every
weekend through the door, come words of wisdom from the world outside.'

Jackson's sardonic, biting vocal delivery is especially effective throughout with outstanding lines including 'Whatever moves beyond these walls, she'll know the facts when Sunday comes along' and 'Well, I've got nothing against the press, they wouldn't print it if it wasn't true.'

The catchy chorus is equally crushing; 'Sunday papers, don't ask no questions. Sunday papers don't get no lies. Sunday papers don't raise objections. Sunday papers ain't got no eyes', with backing vocals joining in on the title words.

Musically this is Maby's showcase; his bass lines are melodic and prominent in the mix, with Sanford and Houghton providing a solid rhythmic backdrop. After the second chorus, Jackson supplies a mournful harmonica solo to which an effective delay has been added. After a final chorus, the song enters its final stretch with a furious double-time section leading to the fade with repeated 'Sunday papers'.

## 'Is She Really Going Out With Him?' (3.33)

Interviewed in *Beat Instrumental* in October 179 Jackson spoke about his first hit single;

> There were about three different ideas that went into it. One was that I heard The Damned doing 'New Rose' and it starts off with 'Is She Really Going Out With Him?', and I thought 'Where have I heard that before?', and it was on that Shangri-Las record 'Leader of the Pack. I thought that that was a pretty good title for a song, and it appeared to me that it should be a song about gorgeous girls walking around with really hideous blokes and obviously it was going to be a humorous song.

It's the definitive outsider anthem, reaching number 13 in the UK singles chart in July 1979, and only just failing to crack the American top twenty. 'Is She Really Going Out With Him?' is a familiar gem packed with all Jackson's strong cards; clever, withering lyrics, a memorable melody, and a universal chorus for anyone who just can't understand what attracts certain women to certain men.

Lyrically there is plenty to enjoy; 'Pretty women out walking with gorillas down my street', 'Tonight's the night when I go to all the parties down my street, I wash my hair and I kid myself I look real smooth', and 'They say that looks don't count for much if so there goes your proof'. Musically the texture is kept sparse with plenty of space, and some occasional piano, especially in the chorus.

The chorus is as excellent as it is heartfelt, and the bridge (2.13-2.46) turns up the aggression; 'But if looks could kill, there's a man there who's marked down as dead, cos I've had my fill, listen you, take your hands off her head, I get so mean around this scene' before subsiding back into the relaxed reggae backing. There's a final defiant chorus, and an understated, regretful coda section ('Something going wrong around here') before a surprise stabbed ending on the third beat of the final bar.

In A Cure for Gravity Jackson commented on the song's appeal;

> Everyone liked it. It was catchy, they said, and had the makings of a hit. I wouldn't know a hit, I protested, from a hole in my head. I liked all my songs, and if I'd written a hit, it was by accident. But I appreciated the enthusiasm, and something else, too: a growing feeling that I was Onto Something.

## 'Happy Loving Couples' (3.08)

Another song with a strong reggae undertow soon shows its 'new wave' pop rock style in the chorus as Jackson once again offers a sarcastic commentary on 'happy loving couples' who make it 'look so easy' and 'talk so kind'. Lyrically the track doesn't get off to the most impressive of starts where the first verse rhymes 'girl' and 'world' in the best Sixth Form poetry tradition. However it soon develops, especially in the powerful pre-chorus; 'But the things that you see ain't necessarily the things you can find'.

The chorus is melodically strong and supremely catchy as Jackson declares 'Until the time that I can do my dancing with a partner, those happy loving couples ain't no friends of mine'. The second verse restates his position; 'People say I'm too damn fussy when it comes to girls, happy couples say I must live in a lonely world' before some clever wordplay; 'Want to be, want to really be what my friends pretend to be, be it in my own good time, being kind to myself till I become one of two of a kind'.

A second chorus leads into a simple but fantastic guitar sequence where Maby's bass pulses underneath as Jackson hits maximum sneerage with a spoken rant; 'You know what I mean, happy loving couples in matching white polo-neck sweaters, reading *Ideal Homes* magazine,' before breaking into another pre-chorus and final chorus. The coda reprises the guitar chord sequence with repeated 'You ain't no friends of mine' until, suddenly, the track is cut short with someone (it sounds like Jackson) saying 'Right, that's enough' and we're straight into...

## 'Throw It Away' (2.49)

...a full-throttle, guitar-led, punky, high-energy thrasher which combines plenty of energy and attitude with a strong sense of melody and conviction. 'Throw It Away' has elements of blues in the call and response structure between the four-bar vocal verses, and a matching instrumental section where the piano is attacked with some force. The pre-chorus ups the rock'n'roll ante before the simplistic chorus which merely repeats the title four times.

The song is initially another attack on the press; 'Wake up this morning and the papers on the mat, poor getting poorer and the rich are getting fat – again'. Again, a low score for originality here, but the second verse is better; 'Wake up this morning there's a letter on the mat, big brother wanna know what little brother's at – again. Life is a piece of paper, goes on forever, sign on the dotted line or end up in the river drowned'. Like the first verse this is also spoiled by the vocals being treated with too much reverberation and placed too far back in the mix. These aspects disappear for the brightly aggressive chorus.

There is an unexpected instrumental section (1.29-1.54) where a discordant, jarring guitar chord sequence is underpinned by some relentless bass and drum fury whilst Jackson shouts 'Among the rule of men entirely great the typewriter is mightier than the machine gun', a reinterpretation of the famous phrase of the English playwright Edward Bulwer-Lytton (1803-1873); 'The pen is mightier than the sword.' The third verse is a disappointing reprise of the second, and the chorus is repeated with increasing energy building to another sudden stop on the first beat of the final bar.

## 'Baby Stick Around' (2.36)

This poppy, rhythmic number is one of the few weak tracks on the album; the instrumentation is light and lacks bite, and lyrically this is Jackson recalling his days playing anywhere and everywhere to anyone and everyone. There are some impressive, harmonised backing vocals in the tuneful chorus but that's about all that impresses here. Maby is given the opportunity to flash his musical chops which he does with some impressive lines in the instrumental section, whilst Sanford and Houghton act as foils to his soloing. Another chorus brings this underachiever to a sharp end.

## 'Look Sharp!' (3.23)

In *A Cure for Gravity* Jackson summed up both this song, his debut album, and his sense of style:

> 'Sharp' – that was what I wanted to be, how I wanted my music to sound, how I wanted to look – you could be sharp even in clothes from Oxfam; it was all about attitude. I tried to sum up the attitude in a song called 'Look Sharp', and I thought it might be a good title for the album, too. Then I decided to call my own label, if I started one, Sharp Records.

The album's confident title track is a return to form; 'Big shot, tell you what, tell me what goes on around here, go on and get me in a corner, smoke my cigarettes and drink my beer'. This raises the stakes in the pre-chorus; 'Tell me that this world is no place for the weak. Then you can look me in the eye and tell me if you see a trace of fear'. The chorus features more word play; 'You gotta look sharp... and you gotta have no illusions, just keep going your way, looking over your shoulder'. Rather than being an ode to the value of a savvy dress code, 'Look Sharp' is a bracing celebration of individuality, resourcefulness, and determination.

Musically this is another mid-tempo, reggae influenced number with a powerful pre-chorus, and a harmonised final pair of lines. The instrumental section is impressive with piano duetting with some driving drums, before some excellent chiming guitar arpeggios merge into an all-too brief piano solo over the introduction's chord sequence. The musical texture is an early indicator of Jackson's later work; his distinctive piano playing will become a strong feature of his post Joe Jackson Band output.

The third verse 'Big shot, thanks a lot, gotta go it's getting late. I got a date with my tailor now, thanks for putting me so straight' leads into another superb pre-chorus; 'Tell me how they run the crime down every street. But check your watch and wallet now before I go and you're too late'. The only disappointing feature of this otherwise excellent song is the throwaway ending which deserved a stronger, punchier conclusion.

## 'Fools In Love' (4.23)
In A Cure for Gravity Jackson mused:

> ...I rebelled against the schmaltz by writing a song called 'Fools in Love'. Over a loping reggae bass line which I hoped was vaguely sinister, I catalogued all the sick and deluded things that lovers did to each other but ended each chorus with a twist: 'I should know because this fool's in love again'. I wasn't in love, but the juxtaposition of the romantic and the cynical suited my new style to a T.

This song is a gently lilting, relaxed yet rhythmical ballad which combines another great melody with clever lyrics to produce another of Jackson's great 'early period' songs. Sanford and Houghton provide a steady reggae backing, through which Maby weaves his prominent bass lines with a melodic skill which counterpoints Jackson's vocals.

Lyrically it appears at first that Jackson has his sardonic hat on again, especially in the second verse ('Fools in love, are there any creatures more pathetic?') and this continues into the chorus; 'Fools in love, they think they're heroes, cos they get to feel more pain, I say fools in love are zeros...' but then he turns the song on its head 'I should know, I should know because this fool's in love again.'

After the second chorus there is a tasteful piano solo which leads into a reprise of the chorus, and a regretful sounding coda with a rising piano arpeggio to the song's gentle close.

'Fools In Love' shows the inherent class in Jackson's songwriting that would mark him out as a unique talent. Musically effective, melodic with an inherent edge and an inventive lyrical perspective, this is just one of many songs which would jostle for selection on the compilations of his work over the ensuing decades.

## '(Do The) Instant Mash' (3.12)
Structured around a distorted guitar riff, which is part funk and part country (funktry?) '(Do The) Instant Mash' is another relatively throwaway track. That

doesn't mean it's a bad song, Jackson doesn't write bad songs; this one is just less involving and memorable.

There are some good moments; the central riff, the refrain leading into the chorus ('It's so easy') decorated with characteristic piano octaves is effective, and the instrumental section has an excellent harmonica solo set against a tight, insistent rock backing. Lyrically Jackson takes aim at three different but similar targets; supermarket 'muzak', discos where the DJ assumes control (a subject Jackson would return to with much greater emotional weight for 'A Slow Song' on *Night And Day*) and pre-film adverts in cinemas.

Unusually, for this album, '(Do The) Instant Mash' fades away with Jackson mimicking the guitar riff. Given the rhythmic spine of the song a punchier 'live end' would have been more effective.

## 'Pretty Girls' (2.55)

Opening with a single guitar chord over a relentless bass drum crotchet beat 'Pretty Girls' sounds like it trips over its heels in the introduction. In reality it's three bars of 4/4 time followed by a single 3/4 bar, and then four more bars of 4/4 over which Jackson's lyrics are, to use his own later words, 'cringe worthy'; 'Ahh, here she comes, just a walk, just, just a walkin' down the street, singing down doobie do do wop, a do do wop, a do do wop, down doobie do do wop, a do do wop, a do do wop, hey!' Don't worry it gets better... just not by much.

Musically the song is an up-tempo punchy little pop rocker with an effective refrain ('Hey, eyes left', and later 'Hey, eyes right'), and some effective backing vocals in the chorus. The best of the lyrical bunch occurs in the third verse; 'God if you're up there, listen to my prayer, in future man should have a different design. Give him a switch so he can turn off his libido now. Give him a tranquiliser built into his mind'.

'Pretty Girls' is another second drawer effort in this collection, one where the music is better than the lyrics. Whilst everyone delivers the respective goods it's one that's best forgotten.

## 'Got The Time' (2.52)

Luckily the final song finds Jackson back on track with another high energy, speedy rocker which neatly sidesteps allegations of punk with plenty of melody and controlled aggression. Lyrically light, the pace of the song reflects the subject matter; 'Time, got the time tick tick ticking in my head'. This is neatly summed up in the blistering line 'If I tell you what I'm doing today, will you shut up and get out of my way?'

Opening with a growling bassline, punchy drums, and a powerful guitar chord sequence, the pace is unrelenting as Jackson spits out his words with conviction. Backing vocals in the chorus maintain the energy levels and after the second chorus there is an aural surprise; an actual guitar solo. Sanford is momentarily let off the rhythmic leash and sets about his fretboard with relish before the volume drops down for a bass solo. Behind this Sanford's off-beat chordal stabs grow and grow into a final chorus onslaught which comes to a sudden stop with a clock ticking away to silence.

## Bonus Tracks
### 'Don't Ask Me' (2.42)
Opening with a driving guitar chord rhythm, Jackson's verse vocals are sung over a bass and drum backing, the guitar building in volume and returning at full volume for the melodic chorus, 'But if you want the answers, don't ask me'. The track is a typical, up-tempo piece of 'new wave' writing which is enlivened by an unexpected, howling harmonica solo after the high energy bridge. Repeated choruses bring the song to a typical 'pub-rock' style ending.

### 'You Got The Fever' (3.36)
This is a more relaxed affair which has echoes of 'Is She Really Going Out With Him?' in the introduction, and 'Look Sharp!' in the instrumental phrases after each of the verse lines; 'Well, things are getting bad now, since your woman left you, you just can't do without it, the other day you even read a book, that tells you how to go about it'.

Lyrically the track charts the frustration of a man who is currently unlucky in love ('...you used to do okay, but that was long ago and far away') and cannot meet a girl who is both attractive and available. He resorts to looking up 'some old number you said you'd never use, and tell yourself you win instead of lose'.

Another harmonica solo decorates the instrumental section of this mid-tempo, commercial tune which ends unexpectedly on the dominant rather than the tonic chord, leaving the song hanging in musical mid-air.

# I'm The Man

Personnel:
Joe Jackson: vocals, piano, harmonica, melodica
Gary Sanford: guitar
Graham Maby: bass, vocals
Dave Houghton: drums, vocals
Recorded at TW Studios, Fulham, London
Produced by David Kershenbaum (with some help from Joe)
Mixed at Eden Studios, Chiswick, London
Engineer: Aldo Bocca
Assistant Engineer: Neill King
All songs written by Joe Jackson
Arranged by Joe Jackson (with some help from the band)
Released: October 1979 on A&M Records
Highest chart position UK: 12, USA: 22

Following hot on the heels of *Look Sharp!*, *I'm the Man* followed its predecessor's template, but with a more cohesive sound and even better songs. Whilst the cover image of Jackson as a typical 'wide boy' showing off a jacket lined with cheap, imitation watches, yo-yos, and jewellery was deliberately tongue-in-cheek, the musical contents were of a much higher and more genuine quality. On his website Jackson described the album thus:

This is really part two of *Look Sharp!* – it was released less than a year later. I don't know how I even had the time to write and record a slightly more mature record, but I think it is, and the best of the first three.

And in an interview with the American publication 'Rolling Stone' in September 1979 he commented:

People said the first album's really raw, but I think this one's more raw than the first. It's a fallacy to think that once a band has done one album, that, with each successive album they should get slicker and cleverer, more complicated. The longer a band stays together, the more capable they should be of getting in a little eight-track studio and banging out an album in a week.

There are plenty of similarities; the songs slot neatly into the post-punk 'new wave' genre, his lyrics range from acidic to defiant to autobiographically humorous, and they are always underpinned by great melodies and impressive playing from the band. Jackson pressed for the title track to be the first single from the album and was puzzled when it failed to chart. A&M decided to release 'It's Different For Girls' which went straight to the UK top ten.

## 'On Your Radio' (4.01)

Talking to the American publication Musician magazine in January 1983 Jackson said:

> 'On Your Radio' is not a revenge song, it's a triumph song. It's supposed to be inspiring saying, 'Hey, you there in the back of the class with the big ears. You can do whatever you want if you just try hard enough.' It's not vindictive; it's much more a song about hope.

This is a high energy statement of attitude; Jackson takes aim at the 'ex-friends, ex-lovers and enemies', former bosses and teachers, and the children who made his school life and early employment unpleasant. Having now acquired a record deal, and being publicly seen as a success in his chosen field, he can finally put some distance between himself and his tormentors as exemplified just before the chorus; 'Don't you know you can't get near me, you can only hope to hear me on your radio...'.

Driven by a powerful guitar, bass and drum backing, Jackson's vocals bristle with confidence against those who ever rejected or hurt him. The introduction features a strong harmonica howl, and the chorus benefits from well sung, harmonised backing vocals. After the second chorus, there is an instrumental break consisting of a guitar chord sequence with a prominent bass line against some busy drumming, before a reprise of the introduction. This is followed by a disappointing repeat of the second verse lyrics; I'm sure Jackson had more people he wanted to sneer at, but sadly the opportunity wasn't taken. Repeated choruses lead into a reprise of the instrumental section which gradually slows to an unconvincing end with some distorted guitar notes growing into feedback and a sudden cut off into...

## 'Geraldine and John' (3.14)

A story song chronicling an affair between a couple ('they are married but, of course, not to each other'), 'Geraldine and John' is set against a medium pace reggae rhythm with Jackson's melodica and Maby's tuneful bass prominent in the introduction.

Geraldine and John play squash together, got to 'keep those bodies supple'; he goes back to a wife 'who's not a lover', and Geraldine can't wait for the next time they will meet again. After the second chorus, the bridge section ('And the feeling's getting stronger that they can't go on much longer, somewhere down the track, something has to crack') leads into an instrumental, with the melodica again taking centre stage, by the end of which time has passed and the relationship is over. Geraldine has packed her things and gone to her mother's. John however bears the scars of the relationship, literally 'from the day he met her brother', but he has a 'happy wife and happy home'. Nothing hurts him, 'nothing more than being lonely'.

Musically this is another rhythmically tight song where Sanford's guitar is relegated to purely chordal duties allied to Houghton's rock-solid drumming. 'Geraldine and John' is packed with great hooks, backing vocals harmonise well, and the melodica (a small keyboard instrument which is played by blowing air through a mouthpiece that fits into a hole in the side of the instrument) is an unusual, but highly effective lead instrument.

## 'Kinda Kute (A Pop Song)' (3.33)

Here we have a guitar-driven pop-rock song with a catchy chorus and strong performances from all involved. It is, however, a step down from the strengths of the preceding numbers and, whilst being full of exuberance, it lacks the lyrical barbs which the best of Jackson's early songs contain.

Here he is 'the guy with the big feet, but plenty of nerve' as he pursues an unnamed lady, both in a nightclub, or when he sees her in daylight. Musically 'Kinda Kute' is engaging, with an upbeat tempo, a positive feel thanks to its major key setting, and jaunty rhythmic playing by the band. After the second chorus, Jackson unleashes his keyboard skills with a piano solo as the volume drops for an instrumental, gradually building into a reprise of the choruses, and a coda of repeated 'Kinda Kute's before the end.

## 'It's Different for Girls' (3.42)

In an interview with the American publication 'Musician' magazine in February 1983 Jackson said:

> 'It's Different For Girls" is a song where the typical roles are reversed. It's about a guy saying, 'I don't want to just go to bed with you — I want to talk and get to know you,' and the girl's saying, 'Oh, come on with that love stuff. Give me a break — let's just get it on.' A lot of my songs have things like that in them, and I've noticed that we have a lot more female attendance at our gigs than most rock 'n' roll bands do. That has something to do with not insulting their intelligence.

Jackson's second big hit of his first era of success is an understated masterpiece of pop song composition. Whether it's the simple repeated two quaver guitar introduction, the steady bass and drum rhythm, the compassionate lyrics, the hook-laden pre-chorus, or the harmony vocals in the immensely catchy chorus, 'It's Different for Girls' has, in retrospect, chart success written all over it.

The opening lines 'What the hell is wrong with you tonight? I can't seem to say or do the right thing' are ones that a lot of people can relate to. As if to unsettle the listener at this point the band insert a single bar of 2/4 time before reverting to 4/4 for the rest of the verse. The second verse ('Mama always told me save yourself, take a little time and find the right girl' and 'Then again don't end up on the shelf, logical advice gets you in a whirl') again throws in the 2/4 unbalancing bar. The song is cleverly structured with dynamic rise and fall between the sections, aided by the considerable care taken with the harmony vocals.

After the second chorus, there is an extended section with overlapping 'You're all the same's as the song moves into its final section with repeated choruses, finishing on the guitar's two-note ostinato and a bass solo. This coda is the song's only weak point, sounding like an improvised close; a fade of the chiming guitar would be more effective here. But a great song is still a great song, and 'It's Different for Girls' showed that Jackson was no one-hit-wonder.

### 'I'm The Man' (3.58)

Seething with energy, the album's title track sees Jackson adopting a slippery persona, gleefully claiming credit for every commercial fad of the late Seventies. In this time frame, Jackson places hula-hoops, yo-yos, Kung Fu ('that was one of my good ones'), skateboards, and the shark from the film *Jaws*.

Subtlety is thrown out of the window here; 'I'm The Man' is a vicious amalgam of aggressive guitars, chugging bass, and driving drums. Glistening with attitude and confidence, the chorus is enhanced with backing vocals and at 1.56 the volume lifts into Sanford's chord driven solo which battles for sonic prominence with Maby's high range bass. The third verse has the narrator 'going to sell you anything, from a thin safety pin to a pork pie hat'. The song builds to a furious end with repeated choruses, concluding on a clichéd drum roll and guitar power chord stab. Listen out for the bass and guitar individually echoing the melody of the chorus's final line 'I'm the man with the yo-yos'.

It's exhilarating stuff, capturing the intensity of the post-punk/New Wave era with conviction and excellent playing. What lifts this track, and so much of Jackson's output above that of his contemporaries, is the intelligence of the lyrics; the second verse has the telling line 'You see I can't always get through to you, so I go for your son', and the third; 'And you think you're immune, but I can sell you anything'.

### 'The Band Wore Blue Shirts (A True Story)' (5.07)

Jackson's recent past and immediate present collide in the introduction to this autobiographical snapshot of his time as a musician for hire. Some light piano-based jazz is bulldozed over by overdriven guitar power chords and a melodica solo. Jackson's, and many other musicians' experiences, are treated with warmth and humour: 'I made a stand for the music... to turn the page with ease, I got the smile that says I'm here to please', and 'Me and the bass guitarist have even shined our shoes, the drummer's shoes are dirty to confuse'.

The chorus is very tuneful with a change in chord sequence and rhythmic backing and strong backing vocals. The second verse continues the 'view-from-the-stage' diatribe; 'Then at the end of the evening they throw the suckers out, don't get me wrong I got no beef about it'. He is paid by the union, gets his shirts 'real cheap', 'I get my money, get home, get some sleep', and the whole thing will start over again the next night.

After the second chorus there is a brief instrumental which extends the feel of the introduction, leading into a reprise of the chorus which gradually fades to nothing over solitary strummed guitar chords.

## 'Don't Wanna Be Like That' (3.41)

Another high energy number which combines plenty of conviction with more strong melodies, 'Don't Wanna Be Like That' is a guitar-led punch of a song with an excellent, exhilarating section at the end of each verse; 'Some people get crazy, some people get lazy, some people get hazy, some people get out'. The chorus is noisy and strong, reeking of 'new wave' energy and attitude whilst never losing sight of the importance of a good tune.

At 2.30 the 'Get crazy' section is expanded with some manic bass playing against the guitar arpeggios, and powerful drum interjections. It is magnificent and uplifting, building gradually into a repeat of the chorus, and a punkish sounding, snappy end.

## 'Amateur Hour' (4.05)

The mood changes completely again. 'Amateur Hour' is a mid-paced ballad with plenty of dynamic contrast. From Jackson's isolated vocal introduction, 'Don't make me... sad' where subtle guitar, bass and drums provide a reflective backdrop, to the build into the strongly harmonised chorus, there is plenty of invention in the arrangement. The sardonicism returns with the final lines of the chorus; 'The world could be a better place if some of us could stay... amateurs'.

'Amateur Hour' is yet another example of Jackson's clever songwriting allied to the well-oiled musical machine that is Sanford, Maby, and Houghton, who play with passion and precision. The song closes with a reprise of the opening two lines and a slow close.

## 'Get That Girl' (3.03)

Another fast track, 'Get That Girl' opens with an aggressive guitar and bass riff, and the chorus; 'Hey you, I'm dancin' with your girl...' full of confidence and attitude. Again this is enhanced by strong harmony vocals and a youthful confidence which is maintained throughout the song. At 2.01 the music moves up a key for a further chorus which only amplifies the furious energy of the track, building to an end which crashes into...

## 'Friday' (3.36)

Quoted in *International Musician* in March 1980 Jackson said of his working class background:

> I'm lucky, I got out. I have a talent. I have music. Everyone has to find their own way of rising above all the everyday shit that grinds you down. Like the song 'Friday'; it is possible to say you don't have to become a zombie. You can make an effort. I had to work hard too.

There's no time to draw breath as 'Friday' tells the story of 'Lazy Gilly' and Jackson's wish that she would transcend the mundanity of her everyday existence, and its regular disappointments; 'Once you clock in you'll take any shit'. The chorus sums the song up neatly; 'She don't care no more, she don't need to fight it, she don't care no more, she gets paid on Friday.'

After the second chorus there is a rapid instrumental section which blends highly melodic guitar and piano motifs and quietens down into a more laid back, reflective third verse; 'Monday morning, Friday's far away, pray you'll make it, it's a magic day...'. This builds and builds into a crescendo with a reprise of the introduction, the final chorus, and a high energy play out which fades with repeated 'Friday's.

## Bonus Track
### 'Come On' (3.29)
This is a bristling, live version of Chuck Berry's 1961 song which was the B-side to the single 'I'm The Man'. It was recorded at The Whisky-A-Go-Go, Hollywood on 12 May 1979.

# Beat Crazy

Personnel:
Joe Jackson: vocals, keyboards, melodica
Graham Maby: bass, vocals
Gary Sanford: guitars
Dave Houghton: drums, vocals
Recorded at Basing Street Studios, London
Produced by Joe Jackson
Engineer: Norman Mighell
Assistant Engineer: Nigel Mills
All songs written and arranged by Joe Jackson
Released: October 1980 on A&M Records
Highest chart position UK: 42, USA: 41

**The lyric sheet accompanying the album contains the following 'mission statement':**

This album represents a desperate attempt to make some sense of rock and roll. Deep in our hearts, we knew it was doomed to failure. The question remains: Why did we try?

**In the American magazine 'Musician' in February 1983 Jackson said of his third album:**

*Beat Crazy* was the first time I really left behind any idea that I was doing rock music. What I tried to do was make some kind of music which just sounded *right*. Everything was built on the bass and drums instead of the guitar, but that didn't mean we were doing reggae rhythms — but people said, "Joe Jackson's done a reggae album.

**Jackson's third album was a relative commercial disappointment, failing to crack the Top 40 either in the UK or the USA, although a lack of a tour in the States didn't help this situation. Musically *Beat Crazy* sees the band moving away from the mixture of styles of *Look Sharp!* and *I'm The Man*, and further into reggae and ska. Jackson commented on the album on his website:**

The stereotypical difficult third album, in which we tried to change the formula a bit without quite knowing how. It's darker than the first two, and the reggae influence is more pronounced. There's some good stuff on it, I especially like the title track and 'Biology' but it's not quite the triumphant swan song of this band. For that see *Volume 4*.

*Beat Crazy* has much more of a 'studio production' feel to it. At times the album is frustrating; there are some laboured, seemingly improvised instrumental passages which outstay their welcome, some of the lyrics aren't developed sufficiently, and there is an emphasis on studio trickery which, whilst being impressive to listen to, takes the edge and attitude off some of the tracks. That said, in the main, *Beat Crazy* presents another strong set of compositions in the relatively restricted guitar, bass, and drums format (not forgetting the inclusion of a melodica again). Jackson's lyrics remain intelligent, swinging between sharp and compassionate, eloquent and descriptive, whilst remaining resolutely set in the social landscape of the time. There wasn't the big 'hit single' this time around, and the comparative failure of the album and the near burn-out of the band meant it would be three decades before these four would meet again on *Volume 4*.

## 'Beat Crazy' (4.15)

Opening with a scream, plenty of reverb, a growling, pentatonic-based Duane Eddy style guitar riff, and a heavily echoed 'What do you want? Blood?' there's plenty going on in the album's title track. Whether it's Houghton's busy ska-flavoured drum patterns, Maby's prominent bass, or Sanford's muscular guitar interjections, 'Beat Crazy' has a very busy texture and is taken at a brisk pace.

Maby takes the vocals for the verses, his vocal style being remarkably similar to Jackson's. The two vocalists take turns at passing views on the youth culture prevalent at the time. Maby sounds like he's a copy of the tabloid 'Daily Express' made flesh; 'Kids today, they're all the same, all call themselves some crazy names, all those drugs, they can't be sane, all that noise affects their brains.'

For his part Jackson provides a spoken word, between-stanza commentary; 'Mods and rockers and Beatle freaks, punks and skunks and kooks and geeks...'. The two combine for the powerfully melodic chorus; 'And it's such a crime, how they waste their time, they can't get nowhere, they've all gone beat crazy'.

The song is unrelenting; reverb adds atmosphere, and there is space between the instruments allowing the music to move and breathe. Copying the 'Two Tone' trend of the time the vocals are occasionally treated with a rapid slap back delay. There's no room for any form of instrumental expression (there are too many words to fit in), and the song comes to an abrupt end on the fourth beat of the bar after a final series of 'Beat Crazy's.

## 'One To One' (3.22)

This is the first song to step outside the formula Jackson had established thus far and gives an indication of the breadth and range of his future compositions and projects. In an interview with *Melody Maker* in November 1980 he said:

It's about how people sometimes get so hung up on political ideology, that they forget the importance of one-to-one relationships. Like one person in the song is saying 'Sit down, I want to talk to you,' and the other person is saying, 'Oh yeah. But what about saving the whale!' Personally, I believe one to one things are far more important. Like you can go to a Rock Against Racism gig and be achieving nothing. To me, that's not as important as being able to have a conversation in the pub with a black person. So I'm just trying to push the more individual aspects of it all.

Opening with a sustained organ/violin tone and a faded-in drum rim-shot, which is the sole percussion throughout the entire song, a piano is the only other instrument used in this sparse, hypnotic number. The lyrics deal with a person (we assume it to be a woman but the interpretation is left deliberately opaque) who has plenty of time for attending demonstrations ('Vegetarians against the Klan'…) but is never prepared to talk 'one to one'.

The chorus is catchy and melodic and throws in a single bar of 2/4 time after every three bars of 4/4 just to throw the listener slightly off track. The second verse continues the theme; 'I agree with what you say, but I don't wanna wear a badge, I don't want to wave a banner like you'. Following the second chorus there is a brief instrumental section based around the chorus's chord progression with Jackson verbally ad-libbing, before concluding 'and three's a crowd'. The piano and rim-shot begin a slow fade whilst the sustained keyboard sound continues at the same volume, coming to a sudden stop which leads us straight into...

## 'In Every Dream Home (A Nightmare)' (4.31)

The introspective mood of 'One To One' becomes a more brooding atmosphere for this dark tale of perception. Again the texture is sparse; Houghton's reggae drumming, Maby's spacious bass lines, and Sanford's rise-and-fall chord sequence sets up a hypnotic atmosphere which is enhanced by the degree of reverb which has been added in production.

Lyrically Jackson paints vivid word scenes; 'The guy who lives upstairs is an actor so they say, or maybe worse... his girlfriend comes to stay, we hear her screams and think that they rehearse, so maybe it's a play, or maybe someone's really getting hurt'. The chorus widens the focus and explodes with powerful drums, loud guitar chords, and Jackson's raw, throaty, impassioned vocals; 'Look round every hometown, every nice house, every fair deal, every good job, every square meal, in every dream home – a nightmare'. The music subsides under the title words returning to the original groove.

The second verse addresses 'the girl who lives next door' who never seems to work 'though the clothes she wears suggest that she's not poor'. Despite the number of men friends who come to her door she 'doesn't look the type to be a whore'. At the end of the second chorus, Jackson goes into some considerable vocal contortions bending the title words in and out of rhythm, as backing vocal 'ooh's add to the mood. The song fades with an isolated drum pattern leaving a memory of an unsettling vignette of suburban living.

## 'The Evil Eye' (3.45)

Some much-needed energy returns. Starting with a quick fade of an energetic drum rhythm and a guitar riff built around the chorus melody, Jackson presents us with a tale of paranoia and voodoo in an everyday setting. There is wordplay in the first verse; 'I got a job in SE15, and after tax, my wage is 16, July the 17th I'll be 18, I don't think I'll live till 19'.

Jackson's character is employed at a butcher, and is hypnotised 'staring into a dead pig's eyes'. The chorus refrain, 'I'm being watched by the evil eye', is repeated although we are never sure what the eye actually is. After the second verse, the music moves into a quieter section with Jackson talking out his paranoia over cymbals, isolated bass, and an effects-heavy guitar which soon builds into the pre-verse section.

In the third verse, we discover that the narrator has changed from victim to perpetrator; 'I got the candles burning low, I got The Cramps on the stereo, I got the doll now I can start, with a pin right through the heart' and the target of his aggression is the shop's customers; 'I got dolls with straw hats, I got ladies with shopping bags, they'll be sorry they crossed me tonight' and it is their turn to be watched 'by the evil eye'.

Musically this is an up-tempo song that, aside from the sparse mid-section, maintains the energy and attitude throughout. Kudos are particularly due to Houghton's creative, busy drumming, whilst Sanford and Maby weave strong melodic lines amongst all the track's undoubted power, supernatural or otherwise.

## 'Mad At You' (6.03)

Another energetic song, 'Mad At You' recalls the 'new wave' strengths of *Look Sharp!* and *I'm The Man* although at over six minutes duration it's twice as long as it needs to be.

The first three minutes are, however, brilliant. Built around an incessant bass riff and relentless drum rhythm, the song is the voice of a man who constantly finds fault with his partner; she takes too long on her make-up, mixes his drink too strong, and makes his breakfast late 'with the wrong kind of egg-cup and the wrong kind of plate'. Jackson doesn't address why the lady in question hasn't taken a baseball bat to this moronic dinosaur before now, instead, unleashing a full-throated, aggressive chorus; 'I'm mad – at you'.

The second verse continues the litany of minor misdemeanours she is guilty of; 'So come on what's your problem, you know we'll miss half the show, how come I'm walking so fast, how come you're walking so slow'. As was revealed in *A Cure for Gravity*, Jackson's father was difficult company at times, and there may be autobiographical memories being used as the protagonist's seemingly never-ending list of issues. After a second powerful chorus, there is a section of distorted guitar doodlings over the unstoppable rhythm section which builds into a final chorus.

This is where the song should have finished, either a fade or a punchy ending would do, but not an additional three minutes devoted to sonic experimentation. Guitars come and go, vocals swoop in and out, reverb and echo play their part with the isolated keyboard lines, the dynamics rise and fall and it's all very technically impressive, but interest soon fades. If 'Mad At You' had been a seven-inch single, this album track would have been the twelve-inch remix. It offers nothing new to the music and soon dilutes the power of the song's first half.

## 'Crime Don't Pay' (4.24)

Starting with a jaunty guitar tune which wouldn't sound out of place as the theme music for a late 1970s TV comedy drama, probably starring Dennis Waterman, 25% of 'Crime Don't Pay' is taken up with its introduction. A more dramatic theme appears 17 seconds in with a distorted guitar melody over a steady four-beat crotchet rhythm which then changes mood, this one with a fairground quality to it. The opening guitar melody is reprised (the words 'Duane' and 'Eddy' again spring to mind) after which the slashing guitar chords of the second theme signal the start of the song proper.

The lyrics take up a mere 40 seconds of the track; Jackson relays how he 'got drunk with a real nice guy last night'. He tells the man that he has been very recently robbed and his smiling companion reveals '...that's the way I started out'. The career criminal has now 'got a nice suit, got a nice car' and advises him not to tell anyone that 'crime don't pay'.

After a reprise of the Duane Eddy theme it would be natural for the story to continue. What happened next? Nothing, apparently. The remaining nearly two minutes of the track are taken up with what transpires to be a fairly pointless jazz- style improvisation involving a cheesy organ 'solo' over Maby's revolving bass line, and subtle drums. A piano joins the mix for no apparent purpose and the whole enterprise drifts off into a fade, which is a shame as the song's central musical ideas are strong and worthy of further lyrical development.

## 'Someone Up There' (3.47)

Another song which captures the 'new wave' power and melody of the first two albums, 'Someone Up There' rattles along at a cracking pace propelled by a busy bassline and energetic drums.

The verse, decorated with gleaming guitar chimes, is understated, Jackson relating a romantic night ('We walked out one autumn evening, someone up there made a fair appear, coloured lights that caught our eyes and reggae music caught our ears'). The dynamic strength increases into the magnificent chorus where the backing vocals, heightened by plenty of reverb, are even stronger than the main vocal melody.

The passion dampens down for the second verse where the tale turns sour; the girl answers a newspaper advert, leaves for the 'other side of town'. The narrator gets drunk and beats up her employer, and that's when he knew the fledgling relationship would be ending. The final lines of the second verse and the chorus are repeated, and the music goes into a fade, leaving Jackson's vocal track in isolation, a clever production touch, as he repeatedly intones 'Oh no'.

## 'Battleground' (2.33)

The lyric sheet dedicates 'Battleground' to Linton Kwesi Johnson, the Jamaican dub poet and political activist, and it is this spoken, rhythmic style that Jackson adopts over Sanford's delay-laden single chord rhythm.

After 44 seconds of this the rhythm section joins in for eight bars, the sound then reverting to the guitar with bass and drum decorations, and the second collection of lyrics. After a four-bar rhythmic break we are into the third section of tuneless words which comes to a sudden halt after the final lines, 'And behind the wall, behind the door, in the dark heat, in the rhythm of the bass beat, something is wrong, and no one is taking the blame'.

Lyrically evocative and musically mesmeric, this track still feels like an experiment; an intriguing exploration of the social issues prevalent at the time, rather than an actual good song. It's worthy, and it's clever, but equally, it's the only song that says 'Skip' to me every time I play this album.

## 'Biology' (4.31)

Fortunately, interest is restored with this highly rhythmic, bass riff dominated, medium pace number. This is Jackson back to his best lyrical word games; the words relate a discussion between a couple. The man has been unfaithful whilst abroad, but denies all responsibility for his actions in the excellent pre-chorus ('It's nothing to do with my heart, nothing to do with my head, nothing to do with our home, nothing to do with our bed') blaming it all on 'Biology – coming in between you and me'. In the second verse 'your biology lesson starts here' as Jackson explains that it's 'not a process controlled by the brain'.

Another chorus, featuring the excellent line 'It's just B-I-O-L-O-G-Why can't you see...', leads into the third and final verse where the lady turns the tables. His confession has left her feeling relieved, and now she has 'no shame about Dave, and Tony, and Phil, and James'. At this revelation Jackson has the traditional, hypocritical male response, ('Baby, baby, this can't be true') but receives the logical and unarguable response; 'Well, what's right for you has to be right for me'.

'Biology' is one of Jackson's great sex equality songs, told with humour, clever detail, and memorable melodies.

## 'Pretty Boys' (3.41)

Straight out of the 'Two Tone' stable, 'Pretty Boys' canters off at a considerable pace with the opening chorus pouring scorn on the 'Pretty boys on my TV screen, teeth so white and hair so clean, pretty boys sing and play guitars' and 'get to be big stars'.

For the first verse, Jackson turns his attention inwards ('How do you rate my sex appeal from one to ten, is my image just a bit confusing?'). The second verse attacks 'promo people, who have a lot to answer for', whilst the third is an appeal for realism; 'I wanna see a human being on my TV set, want some action for the fat and thin man' whilst comparing good looking presenters to robots, 'Just a hero with a smile like a tin man, no brains and no heart...'.

After the fourth and final chorus, the melodica takes over for an instrumental playing the verse vocal melody before a breakdown section at 2.08 where the music moves into a half-time, more relaxed feel. Here the curse of 'Mad At You' raises its head again. The remainder of the track is an exploration of the song's tunes set against various studio production tricks (plenty of reverberation, echo, stereo panning, and so forth.) The dynamic power gradually grows back into the original tempo which leads to a reprise of the opening melodica section and a live ending.

## 'Fit' (4.45)

'Fit' is an altogether more considered composition. Opening with some evocative guitar arpeggios over a laid-back rhythmic accompaniment, this is another of Jackson's pleas for compassion and understanding for people who are born as boys and fighting to be girls' or are 'a whiter shade of brown', people who regularly encounter insult and opposition, people who can't be 'one of us', people who 'only have themselves to blame', people who don't 'fit'.

His vocals drip contempt and anger, especially in the aggressive bridge section; 'That's what you're there for, square pegs in square holes, round pegs in round, you get too big then they can't make new holes, so they'll cut you down'. One of Jackson's trademark lyrical devices, the twisting of the knife, is reserved for the end of the final verse; 'But maybe in some other lifetime, you won't fit, and if you don't fit, you're fit for nothing at all'.

That rare feature, the guitar solo, appears in the instrumental section before the reprise of the final lines as the guitars chime and feedback away into a fade, with Jackson's repeated 'Nothing at all's.

## Bonus Tracks

Also released in 1980 was this trio of songs, appearing as an EP in June.

## 'The Harder They Come' (3.50)

Jimmy Cliff's original slow soulful reggae pop number from 1972 is given the stripped back Joe Jackson Band treatment. The syncopated organ, female backing vocals, and general summery feel of the original are all dispensed with as Sanford, Maby and Houghton deepen the ska in this up-tempo cover version. Jackson gives full rein to his vocal skills in another super clean production. A bizarre sounding keyboard is part of the instrumental interlude; the song is better without it.

## 'Out Of Style' (3.03)

This is a high-speed, high-energy critique of the ephemeral nature of the world of fashion and the pressures to fit in with whatever the current trend is; 'I think there's something stirring in the corner of the page of the *NME*, and I'll let them lead the way'. The chorus is exhilarating with strong harmony vocals and vigorous short tom-tom drum breaks.

The production is sparse; the sound harks back to *Look Sharp!* with crisp guitars, active bass, and brisk drums keeping it tight on the second and fourth beat of each bar. After the second chorus, Jackson eschews the tradition of the guitar instrumental, instead, throwing in an impressive harmonica solo to which a tasteful amount of reverb has been added. Repeated choruses with harmonica fills and a busy rising bass line lead into a sharp end.

## 'Tilt' (2.47)

'Tilt' has a demo feel to it, from its slightly distorted, muffled guitar sound to a general untidiness in the arrangement of this mid-paced number. Lyrically Jackson mixes the attractions of a Penny Arcade with the problems inherent in any relationship; 'Tilt, you're pushing too hard, try just another ball. Tilt so why it's so hard keeping it under control?' The chorus is the best part of the song with a great refrain and strong backing vocals, but the overall impression is of more work needed to transform what is a fairly routine idea into something more attractive.

# Joe Jackson's Jumpin' Jive

Personnel:
Joe Jackson: voice, vibraphone
Graham Maby: bass, vocals
Larry Tolfree: drums, vocals
Pete Thomas: alto saxophone, vocals
Raul Oliviera: trumpet, vocals
Nick Weldon: piano, vocals
Dave Bitelli: tenor saxophone, clarinet, vocals
Arranged and produced by Joe Jackson
Associate producer and engineer: Norman Mighell
Assisted by Matt the Goose
Horn arrangements: Joe Jackson, Pete Thomas, Dave Bitelli, and Raul Oliviera
Recorded at Basing Street Studios, London
Released: June 1981 on A&M Records
Highest chart position UK: 14, USA: 42

Jackson's health issues, exacerbated by over two years of near-constant touring meant that, following the dissolution of The Joe Jackson Band meant that he retreated to his family home to recover. It was here he immersed himself in the 'Jump Blues' of the 1940s and organised a new band in the style of Louis Jordan's 'Tympany 5', playing a variety of swing and blues standards.

The Joe Jackson Band was no more. *Jumpin' Jive* retained Maby, but all the other players were one-time hires as Jackson indulged his influences. Houghton had quit the Joe Jackson Band at the end of the tour to support the ambitious but flawed *Beat Crazy* and, not only did Sanford not feature in the line-up, there was no guitar at all. This was quite the shock.

The cover to *Joe Jackson's Jumpin' Jive* must have sent shock waves through the fan base at the time of release. The image evokes jazz, with its white shadow of a pair of saxophones imposed on a light blue background, with a smart-looking, smiling Jackson on the front. The rear of the sleeve had a weird kind of School Photo feel to it. The seven-strong band are in black and white and smiling awkwardly for the camera, Jackson is in the front and centre; Maby has grown an enormous hedge of a beard (possibly as a disguise), and the other musicians look like they're on their way to an Open University Geography Lecturers convention. They are all wearing white, short sleeve shirts, and their substantial ties are in gaudy Technicolor. What is going on here, exactly? Removing the inner sleeve from the outer cover revealed the following explanation:

When my Dad was my age, jazz was not respectable. It played in whorehouses, not Carnegie Hall. These classics of jump, jive and swing are all from the 1940s. 'Jumpin' Jive', 'We, The Cats', and 'San Francisco Fan' from Cab Calloway; 'Symphony Sid', a Lester Young tune with words by King Pleasure; 'Tuxedo

Junction', our tribute to Glenn Miller; and the rest, all performed at one time or other by our main inspiration, Louis Jordan, the king of jukeboxes, who influenced so many but is acknowledged by so few. Like us, he didn't aim at purists, or even jazz fans; just anyone who wanted to listen and enjoy. Reap this righteous riff.

Fans accustomed to the acerbic social commentary, barbed wordplay, and strong original melodies backed by a tight rock band were completely blindsided by this release. Adventurous, fresh, and vivacious, Jackson easily adapted to his chosen musical diversion, role-playing the vocal lines, and clearly enjoying the music he and his topflight session players were making. It was a novel idea and an early demonstration of Jackson's musical dexterity and desire to explore other avenues away from the mainstream. *Jumpin' Jive* is carefree, confident, fun, quirky, and exuberant.

As all the songs covered are reverently recreated an individual analysis of each number seems redundant. Jackson's vocals are well suited to the repertoire, his raw and soulful phrasing adding a fresh sheen to these established tracks, some famous, some gems waiting to be discovered. The brass and woodwind playing is first class, and the overwhelming feeling is one of cool playfulness with plenty of fun thrown in. By turns breathlessly rhythmic or slowly bluesy, the most distinctive feature is Jackson's vocals, full of emotion with excellent diction, and an overwhelming sense of style.

The tracks were:

'Jumpin' With Symphony Sid' (2.42) (Young/Beeks)
'Jack, You're Dead' (2.45) (Miles/Bishop)
'Is You Is Or Is You Ain't My Baby?' (4.57) (Austin/Jordan)
'We The Cats (Shall Hep Ya)' (3.18) (Calloway/Palmer)
'San Francisco Fan' (4.28) (More)
'Five Guys Named Moe' (2.31) (Bresler/Wynn)
'Jumpin' Jive' (2.40) (Calloway/Froeba/Palmer)
'You Run Your Mouth (And I'll Run My Business)' (2.32) (Armstrong)
'What's The Use Of Getting Sober (When You're Gonna Get Drunk Again)' (3.46) (Meyers)
'You're My Meat' (2.55) (Skeets/Tolbert)
'Tuxedo Junction' (5.18) (Feyne/ Hawkins/Johnson/Dash)
'How Long Must I Wait For You?' (4.05) (Specht)

Introducing 'Tuxedo Junction' on the *Live At Rockpalast* CD Jackson refers to *Jumpin' Jive* as a 'little mental aberration of mine a couple of years ago'. He is being overly critical of the album. However, *Jumpin' Jive* remains the record of his I play the least, although it's great as backing music for parties.

# Night And Day

Personnel:
Joe Jackson: lead vocals, piano, electric pianos, organs, synthesisers, alto saxophone, and vibraphone
Graham Maby: bass, vocals, percussion
Larry Tolfree: drums, timbales, percussion
Sue Hadjopoulos: congas, bongos, timbales, orchestra bells, xylophone, miscellaneous percussion, flute, and vocals
Guest musicians:
Ricardo Torres: bongos, cowbell, and clave
Ed Roynesdal: violin, and synthesiser programming
Jack Waldman: synthesiser programming
Al Weissman: background vocals
Grace Millan: background vocals
Recorded at Blue Rock Studio, SoHo, New York City
Produced by David Kershenbaum and Joe Jackson
Engineered by Michael Ewasko
Assistant engineer: Ken Tracht
Arranged and orchestrated by Joe Jackson
All songs written by Joe Jackson except where noted
Released: June 1982 on A&M Records
Highest chart position UK: 3, USA: 4

If *Jumpin' Jive* was a significant sidestep out of the mainstream, Jackson's next album proved to be a major milestone, both creatively and commercially. Nothing he had previously released prepared fans for what was to come, yet elements of the songs on *Night and Day* are to be found in all four previous albums. *Night And Day* is the result of an artist throwing off any notions of audience numbers, chart placings, or financial gains; someone who takes creative control, follows their own path and is rewarded, both commercially and critically, for their efforts.

*Night And Day* is the first Jackson album to put the keyboard front and centre of its sound. It's a classy pop-jazz-salsa-dance hybrid and 'Steppin' Out' became a huge hit earning airplay on adult-orientated-rock radio before spreading to the pop charts. This song alone earned Jackson a Grammy nomination for 'Record of The Year' and 'Best Pop Vocal performance (Male)'.

Jackson's inspiration came from a post-divorce move to New York. In this musical melting pot of a city, Jackson picked up on the Puerto Rican rhythms of the streets, as well as immersing himself in the stylings of the jazz music which had been hugely popular before the rise of rock and roll. And so *Night And Day* was a synthesis of these two genres, becoming an album which was simultaneously hip and elegant, urban yet also urbane.

The album presented two very different musical personalities. The original Side One, called 'Night', is a sustained riot of rhythms, converging and colliding songs, an unrelenting busyness reflecting the 'City That Never Sleeps' after dark. It's the aural equivalent of walking through different neighbourhoods, and absorbing the sounds and atmospheres of each. In complete contrast, the 'Day' side (number two, in old money) presented three exquisite piano-based ballads, a definitive change of mood, representing the morning after the night before. Only the second track, 'Cancer', with its prominent salsa rhythm, harked back.

The album was not an immediate commercial or critical success, but it would ultimately come to be viewed as one of the songwriter's best works and represented the first full flight of Jackson at his eclectic best, realising the breadth of his artistic range and ambition.

## 'Another World' (4.00)

Speaking to *Musicians Weekly Classified* in August 1982 Jackson summarised his thoughts on the composition:

> What I tried to do in the lyric of that song was not tell a story but suggest a mood, you know? It's just about a feeling that you get sometimes when you suddenly see the light. You can be really low then all of a sudden, something happens which changes your outlook. Suddenly you feel optimistic. The song is about a feeling of optimism. It was inspired by quite a few different events – quite a few things that happened to me. I just thought it would be nice to write a song that conveyed a feeling of optimism. It's not really about much more than that.

Right from the start *Night And Day* sets out its credentials. Opening with a 22-second drum and syncopated percussion duet, a glorious descending piano and bass riff is added before we're into the main body of the song with Jackson's anguished, expressive vocals; 'I was so low, people almost made me give up trying, always said "No" then I turned around, saw someone smiling'. The music moves into a more reassuring, hopeful chorus ('I stepped into – another world') where an Oriental sounding theme is introduced and then harmonised on percussion.

A second verse and chorus emphasise the multi-ethnic setting of both the lyrics (Lower Manhattan) and music. The chorus is repeated over a largely percussion and drum break, into which additional instruments are included. The Oriental theme is repeated and fades as the introduction for the next song is blended in uncomfortably, as we move between musical and geographical locations...

## 'Chinatown' (4.07)

This is a slower, more atmospherically brooding song than its brightly optimistic predecessor. Dramatic piano chords and a sinuous organ melody is used as the melody for the verse, the song beginning with the chorus ('I was trying to find Chinatown'). The lyrics are an evocative, disturbing description of an unfamiliar area of New York after dark: 'An old black man pushed a shopping trolley filled with tin cans, avoided his glance I'm nervous and I'm lost, and I don't see too many restaurants'.

Again, heavily percussive, the track is dominated by the relentless, sustained organ tune. The rhythm and tempo are insistent, and there is a tension to the harmonic structure, which is brought to vivid life in the final verse; 'A guy laid out with a knife in his back, a cop came along told him move on, go home and sleep it off, I didn't know if I should get involved'. After repeated chorus refrains, the music again fades as the album's third song barges its way to the front of the speakers, demanding attention...

## 'TV Age' (3.43) (Jackson/Tatler)
Jackson's vocal style here resembles David Byrne of Talking Heads, circa 1981's 'Once In A Lifetime' in this up-tempo, funk-based song. He dials down the withering sarcasm of *Look Sharp!* and *I'm The Man* for commentary on the prevalence of, and reliance on, the television set. Backing vocals feature prominently singing the first line of each verse couplet, with Jackson speak-singing the response line. So far, so busily funky.

At 1.14, the music moves into a jazzier, dreamlike texture which is less engaging than what has gone before, with plenty of reverberation added to the vocal lines. At 2.0,6 the original theme and feel are restored, and an instrumental section featuring a saxophone solo moves into the final verses and chorus. An instrumental fade leads into another collision introduction as the wildly syncopated piano riff emerges for what will become...

## 'Target' (3.50)
In the same Musicians Weekly Classified Jackson spoke about this song:

Sometimes when you are walking about the street, you just get scared. It was partly inspired by Lennon getting shot as well. People think that when you achieve some kind of success, you don't have to go through the same shit everyone else does. But you do, you know. All the money in the world didn't stop John Lennon poking his head out of a door and getting shot. That song is about the paranoia of being on the street and thinking, anyone can pull out a gun and shoot me at any moment. I don't feel like that all the time, or else I couldn't handle it. I love living in New York.

This is another percussively busy track with a sense of inherent city danger to it; 'Uptown, downtown, no one's fussy, I'm a target...' Jackson's confident response to the warning he hears, 'I say maybe you're just lazy, got to either swim or drown' are tempered by an appreciation of the realities of city living; 'I know what I'm doing, I'm happy day to day, but then something happens, takes my nerve away'.

The carnival atmosphere of the accompanying sound sets up an odd listening experience. Dark lyrics are married to bright, energetic music, and concentrating on one tends to move the other out of focus. An organ solo with prominent bass interjections at 1.35 highlights this differential. This builds into a jazzier section which is followed by a drum and percussion break supported by a two note bass piano ostinato. More jazz inflections grow to a crescendo which returns us to the chorus, and a fade with just the initial piano riff and percussion. As this fades the famous synth bass and piano melody of 'Steppin' Out' hoves into view...

## 'Steppin' Out' (4.30)

'Steppin' Out' works because for the first time on this album there is less going on musically, and this allows the strong melodies and lyrics to gain a greater foothold in the mind. The song itself is, of course, a classic of composition and performance.

It is easy to imagine this as a soundtrack to a film of someone being driven through New York City. The night is still young and alive with possibilities. There is a lightness of touch and a sureness of melodic skill in 'Steppin' Out' which justified its hit single status, reaching number six on both the UK and USA singles charts.

This time the song fades to silence over its memorable central chorus piano theme with twinkling percussion. The drums on this track were provided by a 1979 Korg Rhythm 55 drum machine, which was used in the live arrangement when Jackson played the song in 2019, with Tolfree merely doubling the snare. The pulsating bass is synthesised.

## 'Breaking Us In Two' (4.53)

The vocal melody accompanying the song's first line 'Don't you feel like trying something new?' is remarkably similar to the beginning of 'Day After Day', a 1971 song by Badfinger. 'Breaking Us In Two' soon diverges into a superior ballad, but it's a peculiar coincidence. The song followed 'Steppin' Out' into the charts, getting into the top 20 in America.

'Breaking Us in Two' sets the template for the 'Day' side where, with the exception of 'Cancer', the remaining songs are more personal and understated. Piano and percussion dominate in this mid-tempo, melodic masterpiece. There are clever key changes and an excellent synthesiser solo where a saxophone or an overdriven electric guitar could have featured to an equal extent.

It's the lyrics and Jackson's exemplary vocal performance that capture most attention. His words plead with a partner to try to extend their relationship further; 'You and I could never live alone, but don't you feel like breaking out just one day on your own?' This is unusual subject matter for what is in effect a lover's ballad. There is just enough edge to Jackson's delivery to ensure that, despite the hypnotic percussion accompaniment, we remain involved.

The bridge section ('They say two hearts should beat as one for us') ups the intensity before lapsing back into the third verse, a reprise of the title words, and a gentle fade with a rising piano and percussion melody being repeated eventually to nothing. Sublime.

## 'Cancer' (6.05)

'Cancer' is another up-tempo, percussive song which would be better placed on the 'Night' side, even though the overall feel is more relaxed, despite the constant salsa flavoured percussion.

Whilst lyrically it comes across all very parental, Jackson maintains that the words were very much tongue-in-cheek. In an interview with the *Illinois Entertainer* in October 1982 he said:

> I wrote 'Cancer' as a satire about people being paranoid, it's supposed to be funny. I think it's funny. Yet some people think I'm still writing about how hopeless human life is. When I try to be a bit tongue-in-cheek in my songs, people take it deadly serious. It just seems that so much of rock music is so humorless, so I guess people don't expect it to be there.

He emphasized the message in the *Musicians Weekly Classified* interview in August 1982:

> I don't think it's a condition unique to New Yorkers. But there is incredible health consciousness going on in the States. Whole stores full of vitamin pills. And everyone goes out jogging, has heart attacks, and dies. We all know we are going to die anyway, so we might as well smoke, drink and have a good time. Just as I go into the piano solo, I shout, 'Don't play the piano!' The only things that don't give you cancer, give you herpes, so you can't win.

The centrepiece of the song is the lengthy instrumental section which features over two minutes of Jackson's highly impressive jazz piano playing followed by a twenty-second saxophone solo leading into repeats of the concerned chorus and a fade.

## 'Real Men' (4.05)

'Real Men' begins with a considered piano chord sequence outlining the central melody of the verses before picking the speed up into a mid-tempo ballad with the interesting addition of strings in the accompaniment. The verses are in E minor but through a neat modulation, the chorus moves into B major with dynamic growth and a greater application of reverb to heighten some spectacular octave jumps in Jackson's refrain. Some Spector-esque 'Wall Of Sound' drums, and tambourine stabs, increase the powerful effect of this section. The music becomes quieter for the next verses.

Lyrically 'Real Men' is an exploration of what it meant to be a man in the early 1980s where sexual stereotypes had been reversed, turned upside down, or made meaningless; 'What's a man now, what's a man mean, is he rough or is he rugged? Is he cultural and clean?'. The song's final verse is a plea for compassion and understanding; 'Man makes a gun, man goes to war, man can kill and man can take a whore. Kill all the blacks, kill all the reds, and if there's war between the sexes then there'll be no people left'.

Musically, the modulations between verses and choruses aside, 'Real Men' is simple in structure. There is no bridge section, no alteration in instrumentation or a solo section, the melodies and lyrics are more than strong enough to stand by themselves, and this is another masterful composition, ending on a questioning chord sequence which awaits some form of resolution. None is forthcoming.

The best songs are those which possess a timeless quality. Jackson's commentary upon the variety of gender roles and lifestyles he encountered in cosmopolitan New York City showed a songwriter unafraid to take on complex issues and marry them to top-flight melodies and performances. 'Real Men' sounds as fresh and relevant today as it did 40 years ago.

## 'A Slow Song' (7:04)

In the same *Musicians Weekly Classified* interview Jackson said:

> It's very romantic, about being in a club late at night with someone, and you just wish the DJ would play a slow song, just because you're really in the mood for it when you're being bombarded with disco. It's about a romantic longing. It's not about 'the airwaves are full of crap, I'm gonna set 'em all straight.

Arguably saving the best until last, 'A Slow Song' sees Jackson at the height of his game in this masterpiece of melody, dynamics, impassioned lyrics, and passionate performance. The theme of this epic composition is the desire to hear better quality music, songs that communicate something. Jackson had no time for what he regarded as the homogenised rock and pop music that dominated radio and 'A Slow Song' delivers its message with conviction and emotion.

Jackson references the famous quotation of William Congreve (1670-1629), 'Music hath charms to soothe a savage breast.' in the first verse. This is changed to 'Music has charms they say, but in some people's hands it becomes a savage beast' and the track is an imploration for, in the narrator's situation, the DJ to 'play us a slow song'.

Despite the seriousness of the lyrics Jackson isn't above some clever wordplay; 'But I'm brutalised by bass, and terrorised by treble, I'm open to change my mood, but I always get caught in the middle'. The quality of this facet of Jackson's style of writing is sometimes overlooked, and shouldn't be as it adds an extra layer of intent to his delivery; this is a man who knows what he is singing about. Here is a musician, getting frustrated by what he hears, and pleading for something better. Inspiration rather than regurgitation, creativity instead of inertia.

Built around a simple piano figure in 6/8 time the strength of 'A Slow Song' comes from its controlled use of dynamics and careful orchestration. Jackson's vocals are superb, especially in the chorus: 'And I get tired of DJ's, why is it always what he plays, I'm gonna push right through, I'm going to tell him to, tell him to, play us, play us a slow song'. It's with these words that the musical pressure that has been building reaches a crescendo on the underlying dominant seventh chord suddenly finding its release in the return to the tonic and the repeated 'A Slow Song's.

In a live setting, Jackson would sustain this tension to an intense level, letting the music grow and grow until the harmonic weight is so great that the song absolutely has to explode into the title words. This is amply illustrated in the version contained on disc two of *Live 1980/86*, where the post-solo build up into the final chorus (sixteen bars in the studio version) grows to 22 in front of an audience; the sense of climax is palpable, the musical power overwhelming making the fall into the final chorus even more effective. This point is emphasised in the sleeve notes to *Live 1980/86* where Jackson noted:

> Listening to 'Slow Song' I remembered a girl in the audience and her agonised expression, as we drew out the build-up to the last chorus, she burst into tears. I almost burst into tears myself, but maybe that was jetlag.

Similarly, if this song was the last one of the evening, the introduction's keyboard melody would be repeated endlessly after the final chorus as the musicians, including Jackson, left the stage, just leaving a solitary piano playing this simple ostinato in the single spotlight until both sound and light faded to nothing. As a finale, it was quite the spectacle.

'A Slow Song' is a brilliant last track for an album which showed Jackson prepared to go in any musical direction, secure in the knowledge that his ability to write intelligent, powerful, and memorable music would grant him an audience in whatever genre he chose to operate.

# Mike's Murder

Personnel:
Joe Jackson: vocals, keyboards, alto saxophone, percussion, xylophone, and vibraphone
Graham Maby: bass
Larry Tolfree: drums
Sue Hadjopoulos: congas, bongos, and percussion
Joy Askew: synthesiser programming
Recorded at A&R Studios, New York
Produced by Joe Jackson, except 'Memphis' produced by Joe Jackson and David Kershenbaum
Engineered by Brad Leigh
Assistant engineer: Larry Franke
Remixed for soundtrack album at The Record Plant, Los Angeles
Engineered by Phil Jamtaas
Assisted by David Bianco
Film music editor: John LaSalandra.
All songs written and arranged by Joe Jackson
Released: September 1983 on A&M Records
Highest chart position UK: Did not chart, USA: 64

Having finished the tour to promote *Night and Day*, Jackson was asked to contribute a song to the soundtrack for a forthcoming Jeff Bridges film *Mike's Murder*. Jackson ended up recording five songs and three instrumental pieces which were eventually released as the 'original' soundtrack album. Sonically, the project is an extension of *Night And Day*, using the same musicians, and as a result, the new material had a similar feel.

The film did not have an easy gestation, with the final cinematic version being considerably different to what had been originally intended. One of the consequences was that the majority of Jackson's compositions did not feature at all, being replaced by music by John Barry, famous for his arrangement of 'The James Bond Theme', and subsequent 'Bond' franchise movie scores. *Mike's Murder*, the film, was a flop, although Jackson's rescued contributions managed to get into the top 100, and he achieved another charting single in 'Memphis'. His instrumental, 'Breakdown' went on to earn him a Grammy nomination for Best Pop Instrumental Performance.

## 'Cosmopolitan' (4.36)

Opening with a deep piano chord, a chugging bass and drum rhythm quickly sets in with the piano playing a three-note descending chromatic motif of the verse and the title words. A synthesiser adds the secondary theme which links the verses and choruses in this relentlessly mid-tempo song.

Jackson's vocals have a breathless, throaty quality to them. The chorus lifts with the singer returning to the attitudes of the character he adopted for 'On

Your Radio' (*Look Sharp!*); 'And no one touches me, unless it's the way I want it to be. I know I read the right magazines, I'm cosmopolitan, and I don't look back.' The title words benefit from some high-quality backing vocals. After the second chorus, there is an excellent saxophone solo and the number comes to a close after a repeat of the chorus.

'Cosmopolitan' is an almost excellent song which just needs a greater range of instrumentation to make it truly sparkle. Whilst the sound is very much 'of its time' the inclusion of some overdriven electric guitar could have added much to the texture. At this point in his career, Jackson had tired of the instrument, seeking to explore different instrumental blends, and relying on Maby's creative bass lines to take up any rhythmic slack left by the absence of a six-string.

## '1-2-3 Go! (This Town's A Fairground)' (3.00)

This is an upbeat, up-tempo rhythm and blues chugger built around a rising three-chord keyboard progression. The first two lines of the lyrics (rhyming 'girl' unoriginally with 'world') don't exactly show Jackson at his creative best. As this dark tale evolves it's clear that the character in question is, as Jackson intones, indeed 'off to see the wizard, (and) do everything that Dorothy won't do'. It's also slightly disturbing to hear his raspy, sneering 'new wave' vocal tone describe in the first person the character's journey; 'I guess I'm fucking nearly everyone, sometimes I wonder if I'll ever come'. I haven't seen the film so I don't know how this lyric fits the narrative.

The chorus is predictably rowdy with backing vocals, a decorative piano motif, and Maby's throbbing bass well to the front of the mix. '1-2-3 Go! (This Town's A Fairground)' comes across as another song which would be improved by some aggressive electric guitar playing. The track fades away after the final chorus again leaving a sense of unfulfilled potential.

## 'Laundromat Monday' (3.31)

This song mixes elements of *Night And Day* in its choice of instrumentation, and Jackson's early interest in reggae. There's a distinctive brief piano melody which pops up periodically in the chorus of this mid-tempo groover. Opening with the chorus, which again recalls *Look Sharp!*, the verse becomes more sophisticated with a piano accompaniment over a jazz-style chord sequence.

After the second verse and third chorus, the rest of the song is left as a meandering instrumental with piano and vibraphone doing most of the heavy lifting. Not being the most memorable of Jackson's songs in the first place, this section lasts just over a minute, but it feels longer, and the music becomes muzak all too quickly.

## 'Memphis' (4.45)

Now, this is more like it. 'Memphis' is a solid 'four to the floor' soulful rocker, although the organ melody in the introduction strays a little too close to The

Spencer Davis Group's 1967 hit 'Gimme Some Lovin'' for comfort. There is another bizarre section where a synthesiser approximates a Duane Eddy-style chromatic guitar riff.

Once the vocals start there is a sense that Jackson is back on safer ground; his vocals are treated with a 'slap-back' delay and his lyrics have a greater bite to them; ' I met a wise old man, he had hair longer than me. He said, "Memphis is nothing like it used to be, a hundred dead guitarists lying in the cemetery" I felt a sudden chill, now I'm not so sure about... Memphis, Where the hell is Memphis?'

'Memphis' has the most aggression of the five songs presented here, but again the absence of an effective guitar sound robs the track of some of its power. It's another good song, yearning to be great but remains hamstrung by its chorus/verse/chorus structure. There's no change in dynamics or instrumentation, and the absence of a bridge section means the song starts to lose its appeal after the three-minute mark.

## 'Moonlight' (4.20)

The album's ballad, 'Moonlight's atmosphere is partially spoilt by the hard-edged octave piano melody over the more relaxed sound and gentle chord sequence of the electric piano, supported by subtle drums and bass in the introduction. Jackson's voice is more relaxed here as befits the mood of the words; 'Moonlight, starlight, star bright, I think I see my shadow on the wall'.

After a second, sparse verse the music swells for its secondary theme with a synthesiser dominating the texture, as Jackson's voice becomes more impassioned. This is followed by an instrumental section and a reprise of this new section, and the track concludes with a fade of the introductory music.

'Moonlight' sounds like a demo. The tempo needs to be more relaxed and the piano should be toned back in the mix. Jackson's vocals are strong and evocative, but the song itself feels like it needs more work to become ultimately convincing. A saxophone solo would have added much to the atmosphere, but it was a missed opportunity.

## 'Zemio' (11.06)

Jackson's instrumental compositional skills are given their first official outing here.

Zemio is a town in the Central African Republic, and Jackson's incorporation of an African percussive rhythm and feel to the texture reflects this. The opening section recalls *Night And Day* with a heavily percussive rhythm accompanying discordant piano chords and the bass which alternates between deep single notes and high pitched jazz-style improvisation. A simple five-note ostinato based around the pentatonic scale in C minor is introduced on vibraphone with the bass playing a counter melody, whilst the drums provide gunfire-like interruptions. These repetitive musical themes have a mesmeric effect, similar to the compositions of Philip Glass or Steve Reich.

At 2.12, the drums launch into a steady four-beat funk rhythm as saxophone and synthesiser develop the syncopated bass melody over a moving chord sequence (C minor, E minor, F minor, and a return to the tonic). By 3.39, a new percussive ostinato has emerged in C major, against which a saxophone solo in C minor is unleashed with plenty of spaces between the phrases creating a musical tension which adds interest rather than acting as a distraction. The effect is of a soundtrack to New York, with all its hustle and bustle, colour and crowds which we observe from a yellow taxi cruising up avenues and crisscrossing streets.

At 4.17 an electric piano takes centre stage with the saxophone disappearing as Maby's prominent bass provides a constant groove. The solo becomes increasingly jazzy and discordant whilst still being underpinned by a strong funk rhythm. At 6.13 the major key melody returns on synthesizer, which is quickly followed by the textures of the introduction, again with Maby taking a substantial solo. He doesn't overplay, relying instead on long sustained notes, his phrasing becoming gradually busier until at 7.50 he leaves the soundscape. Relentless percussion and drums fill the next two minutes and ten seconds. Maby returns with the groove, and keyboards fill out the sound until the main theme on saxophone and synthesiser plays to the end fade.

You get the feeling that this hypnotic structured 'jam' like mood continued for much longer as all the musicians involved sound like they are enjoying themselves. There is a definite 'tight-but-loose' vibe at play here.

## 'Breakdown' (4.00)

'Breakdown' is a highly atmospheric composition. Opening with the main theme on a flute sound from a synthesiser there is a steady four-beat rhythm on hi-hat, with loud 'heartbeat' twin quaver bass drum stabs on the first beat of each bar, right at the front of the mix. A sustained organ joins the texture, growing in presence until it swamps the sound, gradually becoming louder and discordant until a crescendo is reached at 1.32, and the music reverts to just hi-hat and bass drum.

At 1.48, a typical high octave Jackson elongated piano melody is added with a gently sustained synthesiser in the background until the organ grows again, breaking off to once more leave just the drums. At 2.40, the opening flute melody returns, again with the organ swelling to a speaker-bending intensity, and the music fades quickly with a repeat of the opening theme.

## 'Moonlight Theme' (3.29)

This is a slightly shorter instrumental version of the original song, with the second verse bars missing. The drums have been removed from the mix, but everything else is present and correct, including the overplayed piano melody. This track has been included to beef up the album's running time.

# Body And Soul

Personnel:
Joe Jackson: vocals, piano, saxophone
Graham Maby: bass
Vinnie Zummo: guitar
Ed Roynesdal: keyboards and violin
Tony Aiello: saxophones and flute
Michael Morreale: trumpet and flugelhorn
Gary Burke: drums
Ellen Foley: backing vocals
Elaine Caswell: backing vocals
All songs written and arranged by Joe Jackson
Recorded at the Masonic Hall, 24th Street and 6th Avenue New York City
Produced by David Kershenbaum and Joe Jackson
Engineered by Rik Pekkonen
Mastered by Bernie Grundman
Mixdown Assistant: Dan Nash
Digital recording system by Frank R Dickinson Jr
Production co-ordinator: Jeremy Darby.
Released: March 1984 on A&M Records
Highest chart position UK: 14, USA: 20

During the making of *Mike's Murder* Jackson had become increasingly
dissatisfied with what he saw as the contrived, layered sound of the recording
procedure, and the sterile atmosphere of the typical studio. To this end,
he sought to record his next album in a very different 'old school' manner.
Jackson and producer David Kershenbaum determined that a traditional hall
would offer greater and more realistic sonic possibilities, and they 'auditioned'
dozens of dance halls, theatres, and similar locations. Eventually the pair
decided upon a 1907 Masonic Lodge, a venue which was normally used by the
neighbouring Vanguard Studios for recording classical music performances.

A traditional recording approach was taken. A pair of vintage Neumann M-50
microphones were hung fifteen feet in the air to capture the full sound of the
band playing in the stone and wood environment. To ensure that each player's
work was captured as well as possible the whole band was close-miked, and
the overall volume in the hall was strictly controlled. On occasion, the backing
tracks were recorded by the entire band 'live', often in a small number of
'takes'. Additional instruments were sometimes re-recorded to benefit from the
acoustic sound of the hall without any 'leakage' from other players.

This was the time of the emergence of the Compact Disc, and *Body and
Soul* was the first Jackson album to be recorded entirely digitally. A 3M
32 track Digital Recording System was used to completely reproduce the
ambience of the hall without any tape hiss and increase the dynamic range of
the arrangements. A control room was built in an office at Vanguard Studios,

with the vocals and mixing being completed at Atlantic Studio B, on 60th Street and Broadway.

The music on *Body And Soul* is a mixture of pop, jazz and Latin styles. Jackson's desire for a return to 'proper' musicianship with a tight band playing simultaneously in the same location was realised, with the vocals added separately. The album's front cover shows Jackson in pensive mood, staring into the distance, cradling a saxophone and a lit cigarette. This image was liberally borrowed from Sonny Rollins' 1957 saxophone album *Volume Two* whilst the title was taken from a 1939 Coleman Hawkins saxophone record. The layout and typeface on the rear of the cover also harked back to an earlier era of jazz records.

*Body And Soul* is a stunning album. From the explosive recorded sound to the quality of the songs, it is a masterpiece. Possibly aping the maturity of the sound captured Jackson moves away from much of the ironic observation and biting social commentary which dominated his earlier work toward a more personal expression of the human condition. His ability to write instrumental music is highlighted on 'Loisaida', and the majority of the album's closing track 'Heart Of Ice'. Elsewhere straightforward pop rubs shoulders with Latin rhythms and jazz arrangements, the spirit of Motown is evoked with 'Go For It', funk underpins 'You Can't Get You Want', whilst lovers of high quality, emotional rollercoaster ballads were well served with two outstanding numbers in 'Not Here, Not Now' and 'Be My Number Two'.

## 'The Verdict' (5.33)
The opening track was inspired by the 1982 film of the same name, starring Paul Newman as an alcoholic attorney finding personal and professional redemption in a medical malpractice case which seems impossible to win at the outset.

Lyrically Jackson hits many marks with each verse having some killer contributions. He also addresses the 'work/life balance' with a hard-earned acceptance, refreshing irony, and a well-earned cynicism; 'Some people live so fast, they're so scared of getting old, some people keep on working, all they do is line their graves with gold'. In the final verse he moves into more existential realms; 'We don't know what happens when we die, we only know we die too soon. But we have to try or else our world becomes a waiting room'.

Musically *Body and Soul* sets out its audio credentials right from the start. The opening salvo of drums is explosive, the heavyweight bass and high pitched octave piano riff is crystal clear, and the brass joins in with the chorus melody. Their sound, indeed, the entire sound, is just glorious. A carefully controlled use of dynamics gives 'The Verdict' an enormous emotional punch. After the power of the repeated introductory theme, the music quietens to just piano, bass, light drums, and Jackson's vulnerable verse vocals.

The verses have an unusual beat displacement achieved by the subtle use of 2/4 bars. In the first five-bar verse this occurs on measure four. In the second four-bar verse it takes place in the second measure. This structure is repeated and in the final five-bar phrase acts as a precursor for what is about to happen.

At 1.40, the power returns with a hard-hitting double crotchet/semibreve three-note riff where Jackson becomes more defiant as the song moves into the chorus. As with the introduction, there is a single bar of 3/4 amongst the relentless 4/4 beat in the third of the four-bar phrases. None of these stylistic devices stand out, or sound 'wrong', and such is the strength of the composition and arrangement these deliberate musical 'mis-steps' just sound right.

Another pair of verses and a chorus is followed by a repeat of the introduction/chorus, with Jackson's anguished 'Waiting's rising above the powerful soundscape. Finally, the song comes to a quiet ending with a violin and bass prominent, passing each other on their respective fingerboards as the sound dies away.

'The Verdict' is an impressive statement of intent and encapsulates the ideas of *Body And Soul* neatly into one song; the recorded sound is the best of Jackson's career thus far; his lyrics are both compassionate and hard-edged, the arrangements and playing are first-rate, and the song is massively satisfying. The good news is that there is much more of this level of quality to come...

## 'Cha Cha Loco' (4.47)

The cha-cha is a Cuban dance step which takes its name from the sound of the dancer's footsteps. Loco is from the Spanish word for crazy, locomotora. Opening with a syncopated piano riff against a steady 4/4 rim shot drum rhythm, the 'cha-cha-cha' rhythm (three staccato quavers) bursts through twice on brass. The next part of the introduction features Maby's distinctive fretless bass against a haunting guiro and clave percussion, leading into Jackson's stinging commentary on marriage.

Rather than sounding joyous 'Cha Cha Loco' has a sinister quality, enhanced by the reverb on the traditional percussion instrumentation. The lyrics maintain this tension; 'You tied the knot, don't bite the hand or it won't feed. What she ain't got, be sure to make sure you don't need.' The verse builds into the chorus with added instrumentation of guitar and piano; 'You can't go back, you've booked the band, so take your partner by the hand' with the 'cha-cha-cha' brass leading into the chorus.

The female vocalists sing 'Baile' (the Spanish for dance) as Jackson sharpens his sardonic eye; 'Enjoy the food, so many courses, enjoy the dance, they don't shoot horses'. This latter line is a reference to the dance endurance marathons popular in the United States in the 1930s. Jackson references dance as a metaphor for a successful relationship in the second verse where the focus has either moved to another couple at the same wedding, or the recently married couple at another wedding later on; 'But now you're here you'll dance all night, but never get the steps quite right'. A descending chromatic chord sequence with all instrumentation involved leads into a repeat of the introduction over which a haunting alto saxophone solo is briefly heard.

After the second chorus there is a sleazy sounding tenor sax solo played out over fourteen bars which culminates in the brass 'cha-cha-cha's again' before the song takes an unexpected left turn at 3.25. This features Jackson pitifully intoning 'Cha cha, cha, loco' repeatedly over a relentless cowbell. He is joined by the female vocalists singing the same words, but in an even more syncopated style in the background, to which a repeated heart-beat drum rhythm is added. A final chorus leads to the song's conclusion of a held chord with some gentle jazz style noodling as the music fades away.

## 'Not Here, Not Now' (5.30)

A companion song to 'Cha-Cha Loco', 'Not Here, Not Now' continues the lyrical theme of a relationship under stress against a slow bolero rhythm. Jackson's vocals here are regretful and reflective and, as with so many of his ballads, it is not clear whether he is singing from the male or female perspective. It doesn't matter, but it does indicate why Jackson's songs are held in such high regard for their universal appeal; 'These words of love, so hard for me to find, how can I change my mind, if you can only lie?'

Piano, fretless bass, a very quiet organ, and a syncopated clave provide the world-weary, minor-key accompaniment to the verse which builds superbly into the chorus. Here the A minor tonality is changed into a stupendous suspended 4th chord in C major ('Smiling fa-ces'), but the downbeat mood is maintained in the unusual chord change through B flat to A flat 6th. The dynamic range displayed by the band is superb with doubled tracked vocals, bass and organ being in the forefront of the mix. The music lapses back into its quieter opening for the second verse; 'We drink the wine, like we were really friends, but can our sadness end and work turn into play?'

After a second, powerfully emotive chorus there is a beautiful, thoughtful flugelhorn solo over the verse chord progression. Initially spacious and sustained with a fantastic reverb aiding its effect the solo builds in complexity as the music moves into a final chorus. The song ends with a reprise of the introduction and a slow coda with a rising piano arpeggio drifting to nothing.

## 'You Can't Get What You Want (Till You Know What You Want)' (4.55)

The mood changes dramatically for the next two numbers which closed side one of the original vinyl release.

'You Can't Get What You Want...' is a welcome up-tempo pop number with a strong funk undertone provided by Maby's athletic bass lines and Zummo's decorative guitar phrasing. Lyrically the song sees Jackson in pseudo-philosophical form; 'Sometimes you start feelin' so lost and lonely, then you'll find it's all been in your mind. Sometimes you think someone is the one and only, can't you see, it could be you and me?' It's not as strong as the soul-searching of 'The Verdict', but 'You Can't Get What You Want...'

succeeds more on a musical level with the band sounding like they're enjoying this simpler structured, heavily percussive number.

Whilst the brass do much of the heavy lifting around the verses and choruses, it is Zummo who takes centre stage for a tense, syncopated, be-bop style guitar solo after Maby's freewheeling bass lines at 2.20. Zummo is supported by piano after eight bars, and the brass rejoin the party for the last eight bars which leads into the final verse and chorus.

Perhaps it's me, perhaps it's the song's over exposure (especially on the compilations of Jackson's work), but 'You Can't Get What You Want...' is the relative weak point of *Body And Soul*. It's highly rhythmic, extremely well played, and has a great groove throughout, but lyrically it's less involving, and the words have a 'first draft' feel to them. This is a shame as in all other respects it's a good song, not a great one, but perfectly serviceable. Maybe that's because of the stiff competition which surrounds it, although when released as a single it did reach the Top 20, so what do I know?

## 'Go For It' (4.19)

'Go For It' is joyous. From the foot-tapping rhythm and the optimistic feel of the composition and arrangement to Jackson's lyrics and vocal delivery, this is the songwriter at his uncharacteristic (on record at least) happiest. There are some great lines on display here, emphasising the theme of 'The Verdict' again, you can be heroic, you can fight the odds and win. But, you have to 'Go For It'.

Jackson highlights two examples of people who have succeeded despite their circumstances; George Herman 'Babe' Ruth (1895-1948), the baseball star ('Think of Babe Ruth and you think of hot dogs and beer, but if he could hit a home run so can you, and your weight is just nowhere near'), and Ray Charles (1930-2004) the blind singer-songwriter; 'Think of Ray Charles and you think of sunglasses at night, but if he can play the piano so can you and you can tell black from white'. Funny and effective in equal measure, it's the high energy chorus which really pushes the point home; 'Is that the best you can do? Go for it, go for it, go for it, go for it. If that's the best you can do, get out of my place, take anyone's face, come last in the race, but go for it...'

Musically 'Go For It' is up-beat, up-tempo soulful pop. Guitar stabs, a solid bass line, and a relentless four crotchet rhythm power the number along until a superb 'breakdown' section after the second chorus. At 2.25, Jackson and the backing vocalists repeat 'Go for it's over the band's power-chord stabs, which builds the excitement and enjoyment into a Mexican festival feel trumpet duet. A reprise of the 'Babe Ruth' section leads into the final chorus, with the brass playing an exuberant coda which drives along to the end, where you get the feeling that the musicians happily collapsed after all the energy expended in this excellent song.

## 'Loisaida' (5.36)

Putting aside the film soundtrack *Mike's Murder*, this is the first fully-fledged instrumental to feature on a Joe Jackson album. It is a carefully structured, beautiful piece which opened side two, as was, and has the feel of an overture about it. The title is the Spanish translation of New York's Lower East Side, with the introduction (a simple four crotchet note arpeggio on piano with a growing sustained string backing) bringing to mind sunrise over the Brooklyn Bridge.

The main theme is introduced after 20 seconds. This is a gorgeous saxophone melody that takes over from the piano ostinato, played soulfully over a languid eight-bar backing. This is repeated and at 1.08, the second theme appears on trumpet. This section is more structurally complex. The nine-bar sequence features 5/4 time for measure four and a single bar of 3/4 time in measure six. At 1.33 the saxophone rejoins for a reprise of the first theme, and by 1.56 the piano and strings introduction reappears, coming to a slowed, false ending.

The third section of 'Loisaida' (2.11) features just solitary piano chords (in a slightly left-field, Pink-Floyd-*Dark-Side-Of-The-Moon* style) to which Maby adds a mournful bass melody. This grows in intensity with first the saxophone (2.48) and then the trumpet playing off each other (2.53), adding to the texture that crescendos into a development of the second theme. Drums add to the drama, and the music pauses.

Jackson takes over with the piano at 3.55, playing the second theme where he is joined by the trumpet and bass for the second half of the melody. The first theme on saxophone is reintroduced and repeated and 'Loisaida' closes on a quiet repeat of the introductory ostinato.

This instrumental highlights Jackson's talent as a composer and arranger. Each instrument has room to breathe and space within which the player can give full rein to their expressive talents. The dynamics and textural contrasts are strong, and the music is evocative, passionate, beautiful, and compelling.

## 'Happy Ending' (3.39)

And the mood changes yet again. 'Happy Ending' has the feel of a classic 1960s American pop song given a modern, jazz-influenced twist. The constantly syncopating drums are underpinned by a solid rhythm section of bass, piano, and guitar.

Lyrically Jackson frames a new relationship in the context of a film; 'I'm in a movie where boy meets girl. What happens to me in this brave new world?' This idea is well developed in the bridge section cross-referencing the 'relationship as legal terminology' of 'The Verdict'; 'I get so scared when I see the evidence against our case, each movie so far this year ends up with someone crying, or even someone dying'. Despite this the overall tone is hopeful yet tinged with doubt, as witnessed in the pre-chorus; 'Do I listen to my heart? Do I listen to my head? Do I look at what I see? Or remember what I read? When I tell you how I feel, do I wonder what I've said? Is there nothing we can do about it?'

'Happy Ending' is a duet between Jackson and Elaine Caswell, who sings the second verse. After the second chorus, the bridge section is followed by a spirited saxophone solo. At 2.32 this is joined by the trumpet in a reprise of the verse melody which leads into a final pre-chorus and chorus. The song comes to a gentle, optimistic ending with a rising piano arpeggio.

## 'Be My Number Two' (4.22)

The simplest track on *Body and Soul* is a song of two halves.

The first section is just Jackson and his piano, with subtle contributions from Maby. Jackson's words are poignant and sung with a mixture of optimism and cynicism, once again enabling the listener to relate to the sense of 'once bitten, twice shy' reserve, confidence mixed with self-doubt. The music lifts after two verses; 'And if you got something to say to me, don't try to lay your funny ways on me, I know that it's really not fair of me, but my heart's seen too much action…'.

The music subsides again for the next verse, as Jackson duets with himself in the closing phrases. This is followed by a short instrumental passage, again just piano, which reprises the verse melody before building again into the second theme. The song seemingly comes to an end after the last verse as the music slows on the final line; 'If you'll be my number … two'.

At this point, the introduction starts up again, this time with a greater sense of anticipation and sure enough, at 3.07, the second part of the song takes flight. There is a fantastic crescendo of drums, guitar and bass as the melody which accompanied the verse lyrics are played *fortissimo* by the saxophone, repeated four times before coming to a slowing, satisfying end, the final phrase featuring a brief duet between saxophone and violin. It's stunning stuff, both in its simplicity and the power of the recorded sound. There's a real sense of the musicians really going for it, feeding off the acoustics of the hall.

## 'Heart Of Ice' (6.55)

The album's closer is highly impressive, although it is only based around two main melodies and Jackson's shortest set of lyrics thus far; 'Take a knife, cut out this heart of ice, hold it high, walk into the sun'. Again, the strength of the composition is in the arrangement, dynamics, and shifts in texture which maintain interest throughout.

'Heart Of Ice' builds from nothing. A steady hi-hat rhythm gradually emerges from the silence and the song's first theme is played by a solitary flute, its tone beautifully enhanced by the hall's natural reverberation. A keyboard drone note (a low B) is heard, and the theme is reprised, this time adding a muted saxophone to the texture. At 1.23, the second theme is introduced with a rising melody split between saxophone and flute, then joining in major third intervals as the tune builds to its conclusion. At this point, one of Jackson's trademark octave piano figures playing minims against the semi-quaver hi-hat rhythm appears.

At 1.55, a heartbeat rhythm is introduced on the bass drum and the (un-muted) saxophone plays the first melody, moving into the second melody, which is this time harmonised with the trumpet. The piano ostinato returns, and Maby's bass becomes prominent, joining the heartbeat rhythm, as Burke introduces a single snare stab on the fourth beat of every other bar.

The guitar takes over the main melody at 3.17, supported by a sustained keyboard tone, and the second tune is played with additional harmonies from the brass and woodwind. The minim-based piano tune is repeated with an additional keyboard adding tonal colour, and at 4.06, it's Zummo's turn to take centre stage with another tense, edgy, and fluid sixteen-bar solo. By 4.38, all the musicians are playing the main theme. Chiming guitar chords at the five-minute mark builds the anticipation and, finally, Jackson, Foley and Caswell sing the set of lyrics three times.

Additional sustained organ and harmonies in the vocal arrangement add to the sense of growth and at 6.40, there is a brief, six-bar coda section. This consists of a huge crescendo of the trumpet and saxophone into a new, fast, staccato eight-note melody finishing on the first beat of the bar and an end to this highly original and involving song.

# Big World

Personnel:
Joe Jackson: vocals, piano, recorder, accordion, melodica.
Rick Ford: bass, acoustic guitar, vocals.
Vinnie Zummo: guitars, vocals.
Gary Burke: drums.
Joy Askew: backing vocals.
Nikki Gregoroff: backing vocals.
Peter Hewlett: backing vocals.
Curtis King Junior: Backing vocals.
Recorded at the Roundabout Theatre, East 17th Street, New York City
Produced by David Kershenbaum and Joe Jackson
Remote recording facility: Le Mobile
Engineered by Michael Frondelli
All songs written and arranged by Joe Jackson
Released: April 1986 on A&M Records
Highest chart position UK: 41, USA: 34

For those unfamiliar with the laborious process of making an album, most are recorded at studios with the facilities to record up to 32 (or more) individual tracks of sound. These are then mixed together, balanced, and 'touched-up' with varying degrees of equalisation, reverberation, and other specialist effects. The final 'mix' is then transferred to a conventional two-channel (stereo left and right) master tape from which the album is finally issued.

*Big World* circumvented this long (and therefore expensive) process. It was made in just three days, although the band prepared extensively with rehearsals and a series of sixteen small venue gigs. At these events the producer and engineer worked on getting the right sounds, balances, and other trickery for each song. In effect 'Big World' is probably the first album to be 'mixed' before it was actually recorded; a neat inversion of a traditional approach.

Jackson takes up the story in this excerpt from the album's sleeve notes:

> The final live recordings were made direct to two-track digital master, and since no overdubbing or mixing were possible after the event, what you hear is an exact reproduction of the performances which took pace. To help us in trying to make something superior to a typical live recording, the audience was asked to be as quiet as possible and to hold applause until songs were absolutely finished. However, we believe their presence is reflected in performances more spontaneous and committed than what is normally possible in a studio.

It's an intriguing idea. Jackson was not the first artist who wanted to capture the energy and edge of a live performance on a studio record, but he was, as far as I know, the first to do so with a silent audience present. The act of being watched engenders in a performer a greater need to excel, and the sense of music without the safety net of overdubs or retakes gives much of *Big World* a real sense of excitement and commitment. It is a 'live' album of (at the time) unknown songs.

Sonically the theme of travel flows across all fifteen tracks. Different countries are evoked in the arrangements and lyrics. Whilst *Big World* sees Jackson making a brief return to the predominantly rock instrumentation with which he began his career, the album sees the songwriter spreading his musical wings ever further. For the first time, bassist Maby is missing from the line-up. His replacement, Rick Ford, does a fine job, and Zummo proves there is much more to his talents than just the jazzy, be-bop contributions of *Body And Soul*. When the album was issued on vinyl it was a three-sided double album, if that isn't an oxymoron. The fourth side of the record was blank. For the emerging CD market, the album had the perfect running time.

*Big World* is an immensely satisfying and, at times, exhilarating experience. Jackson transports the listener across the globe with his trademark sharp lyrics, emotive songs, and intelligent arrangements.

## 'Wild West' (4.36)

In a promotional interview for the album Jackson said of the opening track:

'Wild West' is a song about the American dream and... When we performed this song on one of the small club dates we did, which we did as a warm-up to recording the album, someone in the audience shouted out, 'The American dream is bullshit!' and... which isn't exactly what I'm saying. I'm not saying it is and I'm not saying it isn't. I think this song is from a very neutral point of view. It's about the way that America has always been, has always represented the dreams and ambitions of so many people, and really looking at it, not in an idealistic way but asking the question, is that dream still alive, what's happened to it, where is it going in the future, now that things are so much more complex. And that's really what that song is about. It starts off with, I guess the image of the pioneers pushing west, you know, that whole romantic idea of how the West was won, but also gives it a slightly more skeptical modern slant as well.

Beginning with a faded-in, enthusiastically strummed acoustic guitar, an appropriately Ennio Morricone style melody is played on recorder(!), Jackson's lyrics evocatively describe the pursuit of the song's themes: 'But keep thinking that way and you won't get nowhere, 'cause you've got a right just to get to where you're going to, gotta keep running, gotta be the best, gotta walk tall in the Wild West'.

A rising bassline and a reprise of the 'Morricone Melody' is joined by syncopated drums. The increase in energy levels is palpable and the band explodes into action at 1.53 with electric guitar joining the fray as the music goes into full rock mode. The bridge section ('There's still beauty as the flowers bloom on desert sands, and there's still hope as the sun rises over the Rio Grande...') leads into a reprise of the introduction and another verse. Here again, Jackson serves up thoughtful lyrics through economical writing: '...in the land of the free and the not so often brave, there's both love and money, now choose which you will save'.

The power builds again into the final repeated stanzas and 'Wild West' ends as it began, the strummed guitar fading into the distance.

## 'Right And Wrong' (4.35)

Inspired by a speech made by President Ronald Reagan, America remains the focus for the album's second song, a medium tempo funk-rock number with a tightly rhythmic spine of grooving bass, slinky guitar, and solid four-to-the-floor drumming; 'Stop everything, I think I hear the President. The Pied Piper of the TV screen is gonna make it simple...'.

The chorus is powerful with strong backing vocals culminating in a guitar sequence which is a distant relation to Blue Oyster Cult's 1976 hit, 'Don't Fear The Reaper'. A short, jazzier chord progression transports us back to the second verse, with an extended octave piano melody adding to the texture.

The lyrics continue the monologue of the mid-Eighties American Man; 'So what you think, you like the Yankees or the Mets this year? And what about this latest war of words? What about the Commies?' Repeated choruses lead to the song's end, where a sense of chaos is created as the guitar's tremolo arm is deployed to reduce string tension, the arpeggiated notes fall away, and the backing vocalists sigh into the void.

## '(It's A) Big World' (4.44)

The musical mood changes. Over a sustained chord, an Oriental scale-based melody on percussion and vocals moves into a sublime, rhythmic groove with Jackson placing the listener into differing locales. Hong Kong harbour, a beach in Bali, a floor in Kyoto, the Leningradsky Prospekt, the road to Mandalay, Les Champs-Elysses, Istanbul, and Casablanca all get a name check.

Continuous syncopated drumming, with the bass and guitar playing the vocal melody, add to the esoteric ambience, with the lyrics painting evocative images; 'There's an ancient Chinese saying, always seems to slip my mind, does it really die with honour? Does it really matter?'

After the second verse and chorus, an instrumental section has the guitar taking the lead with an accordion backing before powerful chords usher in the third and fourth verses and choruses. Throughout, the lyrics introduce interesting twists; 'There's an eyeball staring at me, and I know I've met my match, do I eat or am I eaten? It's a big adventure', and 'Smoke a pipe in Casablanca, question all you believe in'.

Jackson's wide-angle lens of a chorus wants the listener to expand their horizons; 'It's a big world, so much to do. And plenty of room for me and you'.

The song closes with a reprise of the introduction, gradually subsiding back onto a restful major chord, as if to conclude the day's travels.

## 'Precious Time' (3.22)

An explosive opening based around the 'Time' of the chorus is followed by a speedy rocker with spacious bass, an agitated, funky guitar part, and aggressive drums. Lyrically the travelogue is paused; this is a relationship song with an excellent pre-chorus and chorus; 'But I don't ask that much, just to keep in touch and waste a little of your precious time.' At 3.01 an extended coda is built around rising vocal and guitar melody lines, concluding with a sustained 'Time' mirroring the introduction at its close.

'Precious Time' sounds more like the Jackson of *Look Sharp!* and *I'm The Man* than the eclectic songwriter of the Eighties. The song bursts with energy and melody, the lyrics are sharp and well-crafted, and the entire production captures the live nature of the performance exquisitely.

## 'Tonight And Forever' (2.31)

This is two and a half minutes of pure power-pop-rock heaven which, again, could have found a welcome home on the first two albums.

Another driving rocker, it wastes no time, with stabbing guitar chords over a solid rhythm section. The chorus is superb; energetic, melodic and sing-along; 'I want to be with you tonight … tonight and forever'. After the second chorus, the live nature of the recording is underlined as Zummo raises the volume on his guitar via a boost pedal for his acrobatic solo, increasing the degree of distortion in his sound. A further chorus leads to an ending which comes all too quickly.

## 'Shanghai Sky' (5.10)

The mood changes again. The two-and-a-half-minute introduction to 'Shanghai Sky' is slow and languid; after a short piano solo, an arpeggiated guitar, a trademark octave piano melody and moody bass set the scene for what was the opening track of the album's second side. The entire song is played out in instrumental form before the words first appear.

Jackson's mournful vocals and low-key lyrics are matched by the spacious backing with only an occasional echoed drum beat puncturing the atmosphere; 'Strange how the world got so small, I turned around and there was nowhere left to go'. The track only becomes optimistic in its closing lines; 'After the summer rain children smile, curious and kind, and the world is big again.' A climbing piano arpeggio acts as a brief reprise of the opening music before the song comes to a peaceful conclusion.

## 'Fifty Dollar Love Affair' (3.38)

Beginning with a relaxed guitar melody, bass and drums, the introduction of an accordion immediately transports us to a French port; 'Oh, the romance of these harbour towns, lights that shimmer on canals, and in the bottom of your glass'. The intensity builds into the chorus with a fantastically twisty guitar fill from Zummo, Jackson's voice strengthens as his character searches the town for a '50 dollar love affair'.

Further descriptive lyrics ('Another taste of cheap delight, street food sizzling outside, washed down with the local poison, these back alleys with their pinkish lights and the occasional cries of smugglers, bums, and credit card holders') lead into the second chorus with some neat wordplay; 'I got shore leave and I sure ain't leaving here…'. The play-out echoes the title melody on guitar before a relaxed final chord.

## 'We Can't Live Together' (5.25)

A sinuous, fretless bass melody over laid back, rim-shot percussion opens this slow-burning blues, with the lyrics taking up where 'Fifty Dollar Love Affair' left off; 'In distant lands, there's no such luxury. You give your hand in pre-arranged matrimony'. The chorus bursts open with soulful backing singers and piano joining the texture; 'We can't live together, but we can't stay apart'. The mood quietens for the second verse where Zummo contributes pained phrases in-between Jackson's anguished vocals.

In the intense bridge section Jackson revisits one of the themes of his earlier work; 'Why can't you be just more like me, or me like you. And why can't one and one just add up to two'. A crescendo of instruments and backing vocals leads into Zummo's spiky solo, the tone enhanced by a subtle delay for its first sixteen bars before being joined by piano. His playing grows in intensity and passion leading into a reprise of the chorus, and a climactic end which drifts away with piano arpeggios.

## 'Forty Years' (4.24)

A similar piano figure opens 'Forty Years', written for the fortieth anniversary of the end of World War Two.

Lyrically and vocally Jackson is at his sneering best as he places the listener in various locales; Berlin, Washington DC, and, obliquely, England; 'Shadows are cast as two giants roam over the earth', 'Here in DC they talk about 'Euro disease' and how the French are always so damn hard to please', and, best of all, 'Where I come from they don't like Americans much, think they're so loud, so tasteless and so out of touch. Stiff upper lips are curled into permanent sneers, self-satisfied, awaiting the next forty years'. The combination of a catchy melody and Jackson's vocal tone ensures that the power of his lyrics really cuts through in this song.

Musically the song is just Jackson and his piano, until the instrumental section at 3.31 where Zummo has a solo based on repeated playing of the opening vocal melody which has an unusual and tasteful vibrato applied to it. Jackson joins with a pleasingly melodic baroque-style piano accompaniment to a fade.

## 'Survival' (2.19)

Side Three's opener sees a return to the 'new wave' style aggression. Zummo unleashes a busy chord sequence and energetic bass and drums drive this up-tempo rocker. It's heavy on the rhythms, light on its feet, and isn't going to outstay its welcome.

In addition to being the shortest song on the album, it also has the least number of words; repeated choruses begin proceedings, with an unusual pseudo-rap section over some high-speed drums; 'Life's a bitch and then you die, nothing you can do about it, anything you steal or buy, you're gonna be leaving here without it'. A short, repeated bass riff moves eventually into a reprise of the introduction, and further choruses and a savage, abrupt fourth beat end.

## 'Soul Kiss' (4.44)

This is a medium tempo bluesy number which tries but fails to recapture past glories lyrically with snipes at the 'record stores filled with pretty boys and their material girls', whilst all 'the hippies work for IBM, or take control of faster ways to sell you food that isn't really whole'.

'Soul Kiss' feels underpowered and overly long. The groove is excellent and there is a great syncopated tag melody to the end of the chorus, but the piano is intrusively busy in the instrumental sections. The chorus itself is not one of Jackson's more memorable offerings, and this is the first point in the album where the attention begins to wander. Zummo has a fine distorted solo displaced by the blues driven piano which leads into the final chorus and a sharp ending.

## 'The Jet Set' (3.49)

'The Jet Set' evokes the Sixties 'beat' sound with its Duane Eddy style guitar refrain, and the 'two-and-four' beat drum pattern. This gives it the feel of a throwback to earlier Jackson songs, although pastiche rather than passion seems to be the order of the day. Lyrically he addresses the mindset of the English-speaking tourist abroad in foreign climes; 'Let's get a Big Mac, get it while the dollar's worth a thousand yen', and 'This really is a pretty scene, could you ask your kid to smile please, sorry, what exactly do you mean? Can you say it in English...?'

Whilst bereft of a change in dynamics or alterations to the instrumentation, 'The Jet Set' passes the ears pleasantly, although the chorus isn't one of Jackson's best. At 2.29, a fairground style piano solo is followed by Zummo giving it his best early rock'n'roll guitar impressions. A repeated set of chorus lines brings the number to a predictable, early Beatles style 6th chord end.

## 'Tango Atlantico' (2.58)

A flourish of piano ushers in a heavy tango rhythm and Jackson's sardonic words concerning a soldier at Christmas who 'sighs again and thinks about his kids and English beer'. He walks out into the 'pissing rain' where the clouds look like 'dirty sheep', but 'at least he's got a job and he knows he can't complain'. The second verse focuses on the 'General and the lady' who dance. She 'flashes victory signs and smokes cigars' as 'he shines his medals up for one last chance'.

The instrumental section has Zummo playing a suitably flowing acoustic guitar solo as Jackson re-enacts callous dialogue from the dance floor in the distance; 'Sorry Tommy ... lost a foot? Bloody land mines, no more soccer for you'. The song ends after a final chorus and an amusing two note bass solo.

However, 'Tango Atlantico' is the third song in a row where the attention has wandered. The thought occurs that *Big World* may have been all the better for being three songs shorter.

## 'Home Town' (3.12)

Fortunately, quality is restored with the album's penultimate number. 'Home Town' sees Jackson in autobiographical mode, a theme he would explore in greater depth on his next 'regular' album *Blaze Of Glory*.

Opening with a slow, solo guitar introduction the pace picks up into a light pop rhythm and sounds redolent of the mid-1980s. Jackson's lyrics add necessary weight; here is a man feeling the pressures of modern living as he ploughs through 'files of bills, receipts and credit cards and tickets and the daily news', culminating in the chorus; 'I just want to go back to my home town, though I know it will never be the same, back to my home town, cause it's been so long and I'm wondering if it's still there'.

The second verse addresses the 'city slickers' who 'kill the pain and relocate' when the going gets rough; people who 'never leave the past behind, we just accumulate'. The words become more personal as Jackson focuses on a seaside town, presumably Portsmouth, with its 'waves and seagulls, football crowds and church bells'.

Musically the song follows the well-worn chord sequence made famous by Pachelbel's 'Canon in D' during the verses. In live concert, Jackson would reinterpret the track by playing it at a slower tempo, just his voice and his piano. This, to my mind, is a more persuasive and emotionally involving version and would have worked well on the album as a small island of peace before the power of the final song.

## 'Man In the Street' (5.04)

'Man In the Street' is anthemic. Straight from the start with its rapidly trilled guitar notes, hi-hat rhythm, and menacing drumbeat, there is a unifying quality to the song which makes it a fine album closer.

Recalling '(It's A) Big World', the verse melody has an Eastern quality to it with its minor second interval in the rise of the first phrase ('I'm not a happy guy') before the corresponding major scale-based descent ('But I'm not always sad'). The pre-chorus ups the stakes with powerful, distorted guitar chords scything away underneath the lyrics; 'But no matter who you think you are, there's always someone with a different view, there's always someone thinks he's got a right to say what's good for you'. The chorus itself is even better; 'So, how do you know that the man in the street don't care? And why don't you care when the man in the street don't know, anyway?'

Zummo has a brief, frantic solo before the second verse, with the pre-chorus delivering the lyrical goods again; 'And if you put your hope in God above, or if you watch the skies for Superman, there's always times when you can see the answers slip right through your hands'. For the final choruses backing vocalists join Jackson's impassioned vocals, with one of them hitting the melody line an octave higher. This life-enhancing song fades away, one of the few tracks on *Big World* to do so.

# Will Power

Personnel:

Joe Jackson: piano, keyboard and percussion overdubs.

George Manahan: conductor.

Ed Roynesdal: synthesiser, synthesiser programming, sampling, sequencing, and electric piano.

Gary Burke: drums.

Pat Rebillot: piano (except 'Nocturne).

Vinnie Zummo: guitar.

Anthony Jackson: bass guitar ('Solitude').

Neil Jason: bass guitar ('Will Power').

Tony Aiello: soprano and alto saxophones, clarinet.

Chris Hunter: alto and tenor saxophones.

Steve Slagle: soprano saxophone ('Solitude').

Orchestral session musicians; four flutes/piccolos, four clarinets, oboe, bassoon, four French horns, two trumpets, two trombones, three percussionists, twenty one violins, nine violas, nine cellos, and four double basses

Andrew Zurcher: vocals (on 'Solitude')

Written, orchestrated, and produced by Joe Jackson.

Recorded at RCA Studios, New York City

Recording engineers: Paul Goodman and Michael Frondelli

Additional engineering: Dennis Ferrante

Mixed by Joe Jackson, Michael Frondelli, and Paul Goodman

Released: April 1987 on A&M Records

Highest chart position UK: Did not chart, USA: 131

In the winter of 1985, Jackson was commissioned by the Daei Corporation to write a twenty-minute score for a Japanese film *Shijin No Le* (translation; 'House Of The Poet') which was shown at the Expo85 Science Exposition in Tsukuba in Japan. The orchestral piece was recorded with the Tokyo Symphony Orchestra. Later he adapted the composition, renamed it 'Symphony In One Movement', adding four other instrumental pieces to create his next album. *Will Power*, of course, reflects Jackson's classical music training but the net result was to alienate fans who wanted to hear his latest songs, whilst in the main classical music critics largely ignored him.

To move from what was essentially a five-piece rock band to a 75-strong orchestra is a brave move in anybody's book. Jackson's ninth album presented his fan base with an even bigger leap of faith than the *Beat Crazy/Jumpin' Jive* transition, and record sales reflected this. But popularity or treading musical water has never been a facet of Jackson's creativity, and his desire to explore new genres and compositional styles was only reinforced by *Will Power*.

Fans were aware of Jackson's compositional abilities going back to *Mike's Murder* and the instrumental pieces on *Body and Soul*, but *Will Power* was an entirely new container of aquatic species. Putting cards firmly on the table, I am not a scholar of classical music. My comments on *Will Power* are written from the standpoint of a 'session' guitarist. Students of the 'Western Art Music' genre, as it now seems to be called, are far better placed than I to offer an in-depth analysis.

The reception from some such critics at the time was uneven: The *New York Times* called the album 'a major step forward by an English composer and performer who has never remained in one place for long.' The *Los Angeles Times* took the view that, while praising Jackson's compositional skill, they judged the final track, 'Symphony In One Movement' to be lengthy and meandering and 'as colourless and pretentious as the title suggests'.

'New' media reviews were similarly unforgiving: *AllMusic* dismissed the album as 'a good exercise in self-indulgence but little of anything else', while *Trouser Press* really went for the jugular: 'redolent with unrestrained pomposity... (a) trivial self-indulgence', commenting that 'while Jackson may be impressed by his ability to convince an orchestra to play his melodramatically panoramic music, it's unlikely anyone else will find this exercise especially rewarding.' Ouch!

## 'No Pasaran' (6.03)

In an interview with the New York Times in April 1987 Joe explained the thinking behind this composition:

> This may be the angriest piece of music I've ever written. It's about the violence directed by this country [the US] against Nicaragua – a subject I feel so strongly about that I wouldn't know what to say in words that didn't sound clumsy and preachy. I wanted to tell a little history of Nicaragua in music that builds up tension punctuated by violent, increasingly frequent shocks until everything explodes in the 1979 revolution. Then the music settles into a sustained tension that ends ambiguously.

Built around an initially quiet, medium-paced and syncopated ostinato on the double bass, plucked viola, piano, and synthesiser begin to decorate the soundscape with isolated notes. At 1.05, there is an explosive double note gunshot-like interjection from the brass to which a massive amount of reverberation has been added in the mixing stage.

The ostinato continues with additional instrumentation making its presence felt, the volume and intensity of the music gradually building. At 2.00, there is another brass gunshot and the growth in texture continues. From 2.46, after a further gunshot, percussion joins the music and from 3.2,4 a new synthesiser melody appears. From 4.10 the gunshots become more frequent until they are dominating the sound under which a timpani roll signifies a new theme with the orchestra playing a climbing, almost jazz style melody which culminates in an expansive crescendo at 4.43.

At 5.06, the music becomes vast, cinematic in scope, with a slow, simple melody played in unison before calming down to almost nothing. The opening bass ostinato starts again briefly under sustained strings and distant brass before fading to silence.

Similar to the repetitive minimalist style work of Adams, Reich, and Glass, 'No Pasaran' is a highly effective, atmospherically hypnotic piece of orchestral drama.

## 'Solitude' (9.35)

Opening with a ghostly sustained melody on flute over sustained notes on the synthesiser, the theme quickly becomes a duet with clarinet. At 1.33, there is a three-note, rising melody from the electric bass with off-beat synth chords as the orchestral melody grows in range and colour. The mood here is reflective and peaceful, with occasional crescendos and diminuendos.

At 3.44, the sound becomes tenser with a timpani roll under the long melody lines. At 4.15, Andrew Zurcher's vocal melody (apparently a quotation of two lines from 'Solitude' by Eddie De Lange and Irving Mills) is heard in the distance. Harder edged, dissonant harmonies are heard before the tension grows and subsides again.

At 4.59, the string section takes over with a sweeping phrase before the main theme returns again, underpinned by timpani and a repeat of the vocal lines. Again, the strings appear, before a new, Oriental style rising melody on the electric guitar. This is reprised by the violins as the volume grows with the opening melodies crowding in, with repeated crescendos and diminuendos.

At 7.32, the music becomes dissonant and angry with a saxophone melody fighting its way to the front of the soundscape before relaxing and the theme first heard at 1.33 is repeated. Harmony melodies on the woodwind instruments bring 'Solitude' to a close under a sustained, dissonant chord.

## 'Will Power' (5.50)

This was originally written as 'Overture for Two Pianos' for Katia and Marielle Labeque. In an interview with *Q* magazine in June 1987 Jackson said:

> The feeling of that piece is one of blind determination. It starts off with a bold aggressive theme but pretty soon it falls apart, it gets lost. Then it pieces itself together. It fights its way to the end, and the final sense is not exactly triumph, but of gritting your teeth and getting over the obstacles. I thought that was a good title for the album because when you do something like this, which has no obvious audience, no real support system in place and no real precedent, plus it was logistically so difficult to do, it occurred to me that the only thing holding it together was will power.

After a dramatic opening with trademark short, sparse octave melodies on keyboards the mood lightens at 1.13, adopting a quicker, brighter texture with a flute melody over glittering synthesiser and violin accompaniment. At 1.52, a short, more aggressive section, reminiscent of parts of *West Side Story*

**Right:** Looking sharp; an early promotional photo of Jackson.

**Left:** Jackson the jazzman in 1982.

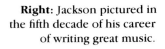

**Right:** Jackson pictured in the fifth decade of his career of writing great music.

**Left:** Best feet forward; *Look Sharp!* is a bristling collection of great songs. (*A&M*)

**Right:** 'Anyone wanna buy some 'Spiv-Rock'?' If so, he's The Man. (*A&M*)

**Right:** *Beat Crazy*. Some great songs succumb to over-production. (*A&M*)

**Left:** *Jumpin' Jive* was the first indication that there was so much more to Jackson's talents than just songwriting. (*A&M*)

**Left:** A *Top of The Pops* appearance of 'Is She Really Going Out With Him?'

**Right:** From the same show, with the bass playing staple that is Graham Maby.

**Left:** A performance on *The Old Grey Whistle Test* with Maby, Sanford, and Houghton.

**Right:** Performing 'Steppin' Out' on *Top of The Pops* in early 1983.

**Left:** 'Going to his place in the rain, on a train'. This is a shot from the promotional video for 'Breaking Us In Two'.

**Right:** Singing 'Happy Ending' with Elaine Caswell in another promotional video. Despite appearances to the contrary, Elaine is not a ventriloquist's dummy!

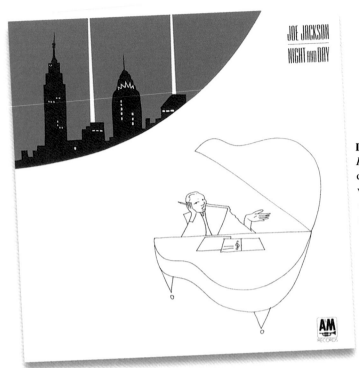

**Left:** *Night And Day*; is a stunning collection of songs which achieved much success and acclaim. (*A&M*)

**Right:** *Mike's Murder* was Jackson's first film soundtrack album. It has the air of *Night And Day* off-cuts about it. (*A&M*)

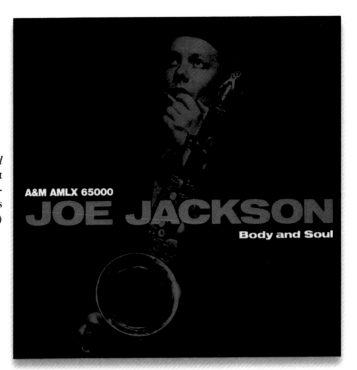

**Right:** *Body And Soul* is Jackson's best album from his not-inconsiderable 1980s output. (*A&M*)

**Left:** *Big World* is a return to the rock band format with another great selection of tunes. (*A&M*)

**Left:** *Will Power* is entirely instrumental and mainly orchestral. Nevertheless, it could never be filed under 'easy listening' in a record shop. (*A&M*)

**Right:** *Tucker…*; Jackson's second film soundtrack album demonstrates yet another impressive string to this composer's bow. (*A&M*)

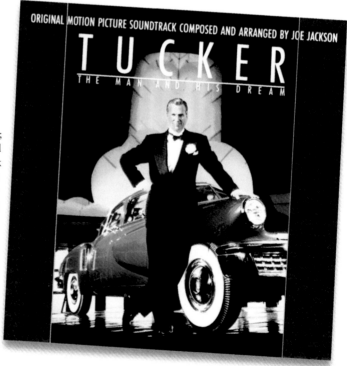

**Right:** *Blaze Of Glory*; twelve glorious songs loosely hung over the concept of an examination of aspects of Jackson's generation. (*A&M*)

**Left:** *Laughter & Lust*. The quality keeps on coming in this superb pop-rock collection. (*Virgin*)

**Left:** Performing on *Later with Jools Holland*, the reformed Joe Jackson Band turn the volume up way past four.

**Right:** A close-up of 'The Man' from the same show.

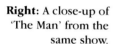

**Left:** Drummer Dave Houghton delivers the goods on the same programme.

**Right:** Jackson in Paris in 2019.

**Left:** Explaining how the drum machine was used on 'Steppin' Out', with Maby on glockenspiel. Yowell and Kumpel look on in apparent amusement.

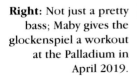

**Right:** Not just a pretty bass; Maby gives the glockenspiel a workout at the Palladium in April 2019.

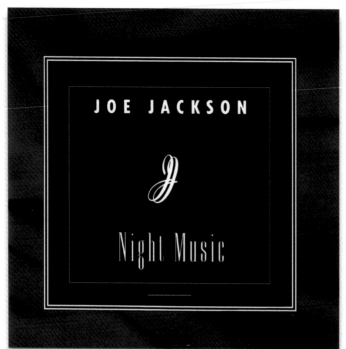

**Left:** *Night Music.* It's an album of haunting, dream-like compositions, part instrumental, part songs, all performed with some unusual instrumentation combinations. (*Virgin*)

**Right:** *Heaven & Hell.* The seven deadly sins get the Jackson treatment in a heavily orchestral work which bears repeated listenings. (*Sony Classical*)

**Right:** *Symphony No.1*. A four-movement instrumental album takes the symphony and mixes it with modern instruments in a semi-autobiographical journey through life. (*Sony Classical*)

**Left:** *Night and Day II*. Some intriguing songs, but overall, a disappointment in this dark-toned sequel set again in New York. (*Sony*)

**Left:** *Volume 4*. No cheap nostalgia trip here. This is a sparkling collection of songs with the original band back together again. It's fresh, alive, and involving. (*Rykodisc*)

**Right:** *Rain*. More high-quality tracks with the same line-up, *sans* Sanford, the album is full of piano-led songwriting excellence. (*Rykodisc*)

**Right:** *The Duke*. 'Duke' Ellington's many impressive pieces receive some eclectic and entertaining re-imaginings from Jackson and some multi-talented friends. (*Razor & Tie*)

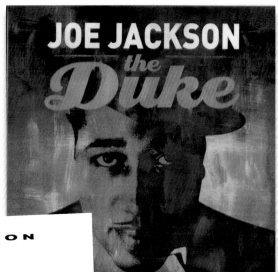

**Left:** *Fast Forward*. A double album of four EPs recorded in four different locations with four different sets of musicians. (*Caroline*)

**Right:** *Fool*. At the time of writing, Jackson's latest studio release returns to the guitar, bass, drums (and piano) format of the first era of his career. (*Edel AG*)

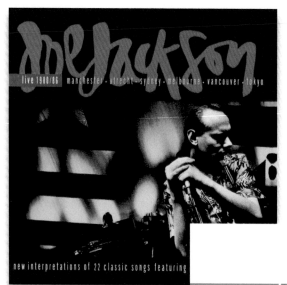

**Left:** *Live 1980/1986*. Jackson's first live album highlights his preference for reworking his songs with new instrumental arrangements. *(A&M)*

**Right:** *Live In New York – Summer in The City*. Jackson, Maby and Gary Burke play a mixture of covers and Jackson originals in an intimate setting. *(Sony)*

**Left:** *Two Rainy Nights*. A live album which focuses on *Night and Day II* with some familiar classics acting as balance. *(Koch)*

is introduced which then retreats as a high melody on the bass guitar and cello appears.

After a short pause, a rapid, baroque-style low melody is played on bass and piano. This is overlaid with chords from the strings and guitar as the melody moves more into the mid-range, becoming more frantic and high-pitched as keyboards take over. The orchestra becomes overwhelming until a repeated synth line is underpinned by a dramatic cello melody with savage interjections from the percussion and brass.

At 4.37, the mood turns to the East with a crescendo as the underlying harmonies move in unexpected directions. Synthesiser and guitar carry the staccato melodies under a swelling string section with powerful interjections from the brass. 'Will Power' finally comes to a calm close of sustained notes.

## 'Nocturne' (4.24)

A solo piano piece played by Jackson, 'Nocturne' is a romantic wander through various musical woods; at times pretty and reflective, elsewhere dark and sinister. Changes in dynamics enhance the composition, with subtle changes in tempo aiding the ebb and flow of the music. It is a beautiful, involving piece, changing in character constantly with plenty of evocative phrases and melodies. 'Nocturne' is, with hindsight, an early exploration of what Jackson would develop on *Night Music* where he mixed skilfully crafted instrumental pieces with intimate songs.

## 'Symphony In One Movement' (16.14)

This begins with the sound of an orchestra tuning in the traditional manner with a sustained chord over which isolated four-note melodies are played by the woodwind musicians. These become an established four-note ostinato which is taken over and then developed by the violins. This leads to a fast crescendo and a rising, jazz style octave melody across the orchestra which dies away to leave a sustained high pitched violin note.

At 1.27, a new theme begins, which puts this listener in mind of a journey by sea with its rolling rhythm and wide-view texture, as a variation of the four-note ostinato appears. The melody is developed on piccolo against a quieter orchestral backdrop. Violins take over just before the three-minute mark and the music becomes more epic in scope.

At 3.27, a trumpet introduces a jazz-style melody and the music becomes more rhythmic and angular. Dissonance appears with some savage cello bowing and distorted electric guitar followed by a quicker section with a pulsing bassline over which a higher-pitched melody is overlaid. As the music progresses it is easy to imagine this as a film soundtrack score with strong echoes of Leonard Bernstein (1918-1990). Syncopated percussion stabs and a repeated six-note synth melody finds the music subsiding again until a solitary brass melody concludes this section.

Seven minutes in, and a new, calmer mood is established with the strings, and a new melody on the bassoon. A violin takes over the soundscape against a discordant brass crescendo which is followed by a thunderous timpani roll, over which a solitary bell is struck repeatedly, like a funeral at a church.

At 9.15, the mood changes again with a sustained violin passage and a pastoral melody on flute. Additional instrumentation colours the texture as the music grows in volume, becoming more passionate as a repeated four-note piano figure appears in the background. The tone deepens in intensity with a descending melody played by the violins and electric guitar.

By this point, the pastoral element has been replaced by a sense of greater tension as the opening sustained 'tuning' chord and the four-note theme is heard again. This builds in speed and volume until a climax is reached with the various sections of the orchestra swirling off each other. Again the music calms with more sustained discordant harmonies over which the earlier 'Bernstein-esque' section is reprised, with keyboards and percussion becoming especially prominent.

This moves into a celebratory sounding section not far removed from Mike Oldfield's 1973 opus *Tubular Bells* until the brass adds a triumphant melody and another crescendo is reached. This climaxes on a sustained, loud major chord which fades leaving the tinkling keyboards eventually dissipating to nothing against a sustained string section accompaniment, which too fades to nothing.

'Symphony In One Movement' is not an easy listen. It's dramatic, at times very dissonant and syncopated and then melodic and soothing. Certainly fans of 'Is She Really Going Out With Him?' could not have known the depth and range of Jackson's talents and, whether you like the piece or indeed any of *Will Power* or not, there's no denying a significant creative ability is at work here.

# Tucker – The Man And His Dream

Personnel:
Joe Jackson: piano, synthesiser, percussion, saucepans, vocals
Paul Spong: trumpet (high notes)
Raul D'Oliveira: trumpet (wah-wah mute)
Pete Thomas: alto saxophone, flute
Bill Charleson: alto saxophone, flute
David Bitelli: tenor saxophone, clarinet
Tony Coe: clarinet, bass clarinet
Rick Taylor: trombone
Vinnie Zummo: guitar
Dave Green: bass
Gary Burke: drums
Frank Ricotti: percussion
Ed Roynesdal: violin, synthesiser, and sampling
Arlette Fibon: ondes martenot
Written by Joe Jackson, except where noted
Arranged and produced by Joe Jackson
Recorded in London.
Gavin Wright: Strings director and coordinator
Released: August 1988 on A&M Records
Highest chart position: did not chart

Prior to his ninth studio album, Jackson released his first live album, *Live 1980/86* in 1988. This was a two-disc spectacular which featured songs from four separate tours. The tracks were:

'One To One', 'I'm The Man', 'Beat Crazy', 'Is She Really Going Out With Him?', 'Don't Wanna Be Like That', 'Got The Time', 'On The Radio', 'Fools In Love', 'Cancer', 'Is She Really Going Out With Him?' (A Cappella Version), 'Look Sharp!', 'Sunday Papers', 'Real Men', 'Is She Really Going Out With Him?' (Acoustic Version), 'Memphis', 'A Slow Song', 'Be My Number Two', 'Breaking Us In Two', 'It's Different For Girls', 'You Can't Get What You Want (Til You Know What You Want)', 'Jumpin' Jive', 'Steppin' Out'

'One To One' to 'Beat Crazy' were taken from the final gig of the Joe Jackson Band on the *Beat Crazy* tour in 1980. 'On The Radio' to 'Look Sharp!' were recorded on the *Night And Day* tour of 1982/3. 'Sunday Papers' to 'A Slow Song' came from the 1984 tour to promote *Body And Soul*. The remaining tracks were taken from the *Big World* tour in 1986.

Writing in the sleeve notes for the album Jackson noted:

...it would be a real live album. Nothing would be re-recorded, overdubbed, or 'fixed' ... it would be devoted to the re-workings of songs, the spontaneous moments, anything that made those concerts something different and apart from the records.

*Tucker – The Man And His Dream* is the soundtrack for the Francis Ford Coppola film of the same title. The album earned Jackson a Grammy nomination for 'Best Album of Original Instrumental Background Score written for a Motion Picture or TV'. The film is a 1988 American biographical drama of Preston Tucker, and his attempt to produce and market the 1948 Tucker Sedan, which was beset by scandal and accusations of stock fraud from the United States Securities and Exchange Commission.

The problem with any 'soundtrack' album is that without the context of the visuals, the characters or the plot the music drifts by without an anchoring point. The story and its participants are key to an understanding and full appreciation of the accompanying music, and without those we are left with the songs and instrumentals to enjoy or ignore in isolation. If you are familiar with the production the music makes sense; on its own the album stands or falls on its own merits.

## 'Captain Of Industry (Overture)' (2.32)
This is a bright and uplifting instrumental featuring both swirling and plucked strings over a brisk tempo, typical of the 'golden age' of Hollywood movies and musicals.

## 'The Car Of Tomorrow – Today!' (1.33)
Another instrumental, this is the first track to sound like it could have appeared on *Jumping Jive*. It is a riot of brass, fast rhythms and a manic jazz guitar solo before an abrupt change of mood into something spookier and more surreal 28 seconds in. This section mixes soaring violins, sustained chords, a slow tempo, and some science fiction-style sound effects behind a sparse melody. At 1.08, and as if nothing unusual has happened, the opening music returns leading to a slower overlaid brass coda.

## 'No Chance Blues' (2.30)
And very bluesy it is, with a slow, loping tempo and a relaxed guitar, bass and drum rhythm section against the woodwind melodies. There is some fantastic clarinet playing which is interspersed with some bar-style piano before the music quietens and slows at the 1.55 mark. This leads to a coda section where just the piano picks out the initial melody in sparse phrases.

## '(He's A) Shape in A Drape' (2.59)
An amused 'One, two, three, four' introduction leads into another bouncy blues number, and the first appearance of Jackson's vocals and, again, we are in *Jumpin' Jive* territory. Backing singers echo Jackson's title vocals adding to the sense of fun permeating the track. At 1.53, the music steps up a gear with a

Glenn Miller tribute section which leads into a full-blown sax solo under which the brass provides a typical bluesy accompaniment and a tightly arranged snappy ending.

## 'Factory' (1.08)
Jazz drums are the main feature of this short instrumental, with fragmented percussion and timpani re-creating the sounds and feel of a factory production line.

## 'Vera' (2.30)
A slow piano introduction leads into a ballad instrumental which feels like it could have fallen off the back of a Stephen Sondheim musical. The mixture of synthesiser and strings is very effective, with the second section melody being taken by the woodwind. Gentle guitar lines also feature in this atmospheric track, and 'Vera' is a beautiful piece of music.

## 'It Pays to Advertise' (0.41)
This is another bluesy jazz instrumental with a full texture further decorated by tuned percussion. The ending features a repeated bass phrase fading to nothing.

## 'Tiger Rag' (2.09) (DaCosta, Edwards, LaRocca, Sharbaro, Shields)
It's *Jumpin' Jive* time yet again for this, the only song on the album not written by Jackson.

'Tiger Rag' is taken at a furiously fast tempo with the off-beat snare drum holding everything together. Beyond the opening verses ('Hold that tiger' and 'Where's that tiger?') sung by anguished sounding vocalists, the rest of the track is, again, instrumental.

Zummo has a suitably frantic solo between 0.27 and 0.40. The brass section then takes over reprising the vocal melody before amusing interjections between wind instruments and, erm, saucepans add a feel of 1920s 'silent comedy' accompaniment. Zummo is back for another chase around the fretboard at 1.20 as the bass player keeps up with admirable aplomb. Jackson 'scat' sings along in the closing section, which comes to a chaotic and surprising ending. 'Tiger Rag' is massively entertaining and sounds like a lot of fun was had in the recording studio.

## 'Showtime In Chicago' (2.45)
The 'big band' feel is re-established for 'Showtime in Chicago' with overlaid brass melodies against an energetic rhythm section, although the mood is more relaxed than 'Tiger Rag'. Another driving bluesy jazz number, this instrumental also features 'car-horn' notes from the brass as well as a superb, muted trumpet solo. The track comes to a subdued close with a sustained low note and a syncopated hi-hat rhythm.

### 'Lone Bank Loan Blues' (1.11)

This has a George Gershwin (1898-1937) feel to it with the soaring clarinet solo over bluesy woodwind backing harking back to 'Rhapsody in Blue' (1924). At 52 seconds, a new theme is briefly introduced before the music comes to an early, doubtful sounding ending.

### 'Speedway' (2.40)

More 'factory' sound effects open this track. Drums and percussion feature heavily before the bass joins, finally building to a fast, big band number. A spectacular clarinet solo appears 52 seconds in, before the main theme is reprised leading into a syncopated brass-driven section. A discordant woodwind melody over a heavy bass drum rhythm drives the track along before the music retreats to just the timpani and drums, lightening in sound. The full band reappears at 2.28 for a brief coda.

### 'Marilee' (3.00)

A solo, mournful jazz piano signals an abrupt mood change. 'Marilee' has a beautiful, late-night bar feel to it with a flowing melody over a relaxed jazz chord progression. At 1.20, the pace quickens slightly as a marimba takes over the melody and bass adds weight at the bottom end. At 1.55, the solo piano returns, bringing the music to its conclusion.

### 'Hangin' In Howard Hughes' Hanger' (2.35)

The Sci-Fi effects return with timpani and marimba over which a slow, rising and falling synthesiser and violin melody create a tense, foreboding atmosphere.

### 'Toast Of the Town' (1.23)

This track has another show overture/opening credits of a film credits feel to it. It's another brass led, up-tempo instrumental which breaks into a samba section 25 seconds in. Here a low string and piano melody play off each other until the big-band swing feel returns at 0.50. This leads to a reprise of the opening, this time with this tune continuing to the end.

### 'Abe's Blues' (2.39)

This is led by the clarinet and is another darkly moody, end-of-the-night feel instrumental. A slow, bluesy piano takes centre stage after 34 seconds and plays the piece out to a fade.

### 'The Trial' (6.44)

The longest track on the album opens with some funeral-esque brass harmonies, which pick up a swing beat 38 seconds in with some light percussion. Strings and piano take over as complex harmonies build with tasteful saxophone adding to the atmospheric texture. Dynamics rise and fall and by the 2.12 mark there are elements of John Barry's 'Bond' film themes from the brass.

The music subsides again, becoming more strictly rhythmic at 2.30 as clarinet and saxophone duet and a muted trumpet plays phrases off against them. Violins swirl, and, at 3.16, Zummo plays a classy lower-range solo as the swing feel returns. The moody feel continues, as do the 'Bond' moments, before a muted trumpet plays suitably anguished phrases in-between loud passages from the brass.

At 5.10 the 'Sci-Fi synth' returns with a cheesy sounding melody which, over the established swing rhythm, sounds downright weird. The brass soon swamps this as the music becomes louder and more celebratory, supported by climbing melodic lines from the violins. The opening theme is reprised at a quieter volume with plucked strings, and the piece ends on an unresolved, syncopated chord.

## 'Freedom Swing/Tucker Jingle' (1.38) (Jackson/Coppola)

'Freedom Swing/Tucker Jingle' is a happy sounding instrumental which combines synthesised voices with traditional instrumentation against another swing rhythm. A saxophone melody provides contrast at 0.34, with the music growing in stature by the one-minute mark into the 'Tucker Jingle' section (which was written by the film director's father, Carmine Coppola.) This is quicker with another joyful, short melody which is played twice, leading to a quick end.

## 'Rhythm Delivery' (3.24)

We return to *Jumpin' Jive* territory one more time for the album's final track. This is another fast instrumental with sufficient space for all the musicians to display their talents, especially Zummo who has two solo sections where he tears up and down the fretboard in a stylish, dramatic fashion. Jackson demonstrates his undoubted jazz piano 'chops' over 32 bars.

At 1.46, a walking bass line ushers in the second part of the track, where vocals are heard again against a rapid rhythmic backing; 'I'm gonna ring your bell because I got your number. I'm gonna knock as well, we got a rhythm delivery'. A key change signals the beginning of a suitably manic sax solo as the band's volume grows and grows. There is another section of verses; 'Yes, I'm gonna rock your soul, you will go to high from low, you from swell will go to hip, but honey, don't forget my tip', before the band round things off with a typically syncopated big band ending.

# Blaze Of Glory

Personnel:
Joe Jackson: lead and backing vocals, organ, piano, fake harmonica, synthesiser
Graham Maby: bass, lead and backing vocals
Steve Elsen: alto saxophone, baritone saxophone
Ed Roynesdal: synthesiser, fake piano, vibraphone, organ, synth piano, violin
Tom Teeley: electric guitar, backing vocals
Charlie Gordon: trombone
Sue Hadjopoulos: congas
Chris Hunter: alto saxophone
Gary Burke: drums
Tony Barrero: trumpet
Michael Morreale: trumpet
Vinnie Zummo: acoustic, electric, and nylon-strung guitars, electric sitar
Joy Askew: lead and backing vocals
Rick Ford: bass, fretless bass
Drew Barfield: lead and backing vocals
Tony Aiello: flute, tenor saxophone
Anthony Cox: acoustic bass ('Blaze Of Glory')
Glenn Dicterow: violin ('Sentimental Thing')
Charles McCracken: cello ('The Human Touch')
Conductor: Gene Orloff ('Sentimental Thing')
Written, arranged, and produced by Joe Jackson
Associate producer: Ed Roynesdal
Recorded at Bearsville Studios, New York State; November/December 1988
Engineered by Joe Barbaria
Assisted by Thom Cadley
Mixed at Electric Lady, New York City, January 1989
Assisted by Bridget Daly
Strings on 'Sentimental Thing' recorded by Paul Goodman at RCA Studios, NYC
Digital editing by Scott Hull at Masterdisk
Direct metal mastering by Bob Ludwig at Masterdisk
Released: April 1989 on A&M Records
Highest chart position UK: 36, USA: 61

The spring of 1989 saw Jackson return with his songwriting skills fully lit.
*Blaze Of Glory* contained twelve songs which embraced the concept of 'his
generation', to whom the record was dedicated. The subject matter ranged from
the optimism of the 1950s ('Tomorrow's World'), to the politics of terrorism
('Rant And Rave'), and the Cold War ('Evil Empire'). Moving from political to
social commentary Jackson also took swipes at rockers who had passed their
integrity date ('Nineteen Forever'), and the 'Yuppie' movement of the late 1980s
('Discipline'). There was also space for three excellent ballads, and, surprisingly,
a Greek influenced instrumental. Writing on his website Jackson reflected:

Like *Big World* this is a diverse record which I tried to tie together with an overall theme. In *Big World* it was travel, and this time it was a journey through life, from childhood to some sort of vaguely defined maturity. I think it's a stronger album than the previous two. It has a kind of epic quality with a 16-piece band. For the tour I cut it down to a mere 11. I still lost money.

The near-continuous flow of song into song helps cement the theme of a 'journey through life'. Whilst each track is a standalone number the transitions between them are seamless, and this gives the album a well-integrated feel. And, for the first time since *Body And Soul*, there is a real sense that Jackson is back to what he does best. The songs are imaginative, melodic, and memorable. The arrangements are intricate, and the playing is masterful; there is a great sense of élan in amongst all this creativity, and the range and breadth of the compositions is hugely impressive.

## 'Tomorrow's World' (4.30)
There's a strong feeling of optimism and energy to 'Tomorrow's World', capturing the hope of better times ahead. Enthusiasm for the future and its anticipated benefits are demonstrated in the breathless vocal style, the exuberant playing, the bright, lively-sounding production, and the idealistic lyrics, examples including; 'There'll be cities on the moon', 'We'll live on power from the sun', and 'There'll be food for everyone'.

Reference is made to the 'Voyager' probes (1977) in the conversational second verse; 'D'you remember that rocket they blasted into God knows where? With the pictures for someone to find? With chemical symbols saying "Hi, how you doin'?" to the folks out there?' The final line is telling; 'Yeah they put the Bach music in, left all the shit behind'.

The song opens quietly with a repeated keyboard ostinato and a relentless rim-shot drum rhythm. Plenty of reverberation adds to the sense of wonder in the vocals, and a loud guitar and bass sequence explodes with 'They're going to build a ship to take us there'. The volume subsides, lifting again with the guitar and bass moving into the chorus which lifts the mood even further. Dynamic and textural changes like this illustrate just how good Jackson is at crafting music to move our emotions. This is uplifting and hopeful, as well as rocking along at a cracking pace. After a second chorus, there is a pleasing carillon of overlapping keyboard melodies before the returning chorus cranks the volume up again. The song closes with some clashing chords where a new, repeated two-string guitar ostinato appears amid the harmonised 'Tomorrow's World's. This fades into the ether, as the guitar melody becomes the link to the next track.

## 'Me And You (Against the World)' (4.14)
'Me And You (Against the World)' recalls the power and brio of the first two Joe Jackson Band albums, except here the music is enhanced by a boisterous

brass section. The track brings the listener back down to earth, as it were, with Jackson's words being more personal. This is another lyric of hope and enthusiasm, this time for a new relationship. This mood is summed up best in the high energy bridge section which follows the excellent sing-along chorus; 'I've read the Bible and those books at school, but they don't make much sense of this. The finest minds are calling me a fool, but you destroy them with your kiss, just one kiss'.

Despite all this 'new wave' style energy, just where a guitar solo might be expected, we get a repeat of the introductory brass melody with an interweaving swirly keyboard tune before Jackson's simple yet distinctively effective piano solo. The pace and volume don't let up, and the song powers along to its conclusion with the rotating keyboard melody suddenly speeding up and changing key, forming the background for the atmospheric introduction to one of Jackson's finest songs...

## 'Down To London' (4.14)

Lyrically 'Down To London' is 'sortobiographical', immediately contrasting the 'death rattle of this rusty old town' (probably a reference to Portsmouth) with his move to London with its 'sound of laughter all along the Thames', where he wants to see 'life after ten at night'.

Riding along on a jaunty piano riff, with a very prominent tambourine on beats two and four of each bar, and a steady tempo drum rhythm, 'Down To London' is another song capturing anticipation and expectation. The chorus is superb with a sleazy electric guitar riff and excellent, harmonised backing vocals; 'So if they ask you where I am, I'm in the back of a Transit Van, in a squat on the Earls Court Road, gone down to London turning coal into gold'. Jackson's ambition is revealed in its repeated final lines; 'Gone down to London to be the king'.

The second verse is a sung conversation between Jackson and an unnamed female character with a similar attitude; 'The boys back home all seem to look the same' and 'You should stick with me, one of us will make it, just you see'. After a particularly evocative verse which will resonate with all musicians ('Hey, can you hear me back there, or is there anybody left to care?'), the second chorus references Soho bars and busking on the underground. This is followed by a harmonica solo with significant support from the brass and then a third chorus (with its 'Kings Cross caff, and leather jackets') before finally finishing, after a reprise of the harmonica and brass instrumental section, on a sustained sub-dominant chord which blends smoothly into...

## 'Sentimental Thing' (6.09)

After three upbeat anthems of youthful enthusiasm and aspiration, the mood spirals down in this string-dominated ballad of regret at the end of an intense relationship. Aside from some sporadic electric guitar and synthesiser phrases the soundscape is dominated by an orchestra which supports Jackson's anguished vocal lines; 'And after all the confrontations, when it comes for saying goodbye, all that I can wonder is what do I do with these flowers? And what do I do with my evenings? And what do you do with that ring?'.

Three minutes in there is a change of feel as the volume quietens and Glenn Dicterow's solo violin line soars and dives over the string accompaniment. There is a subtle, repeated single note on electric guitar in a syncopated rhythm which will become more apparent as the transition into the next track.

At 4.48 the song appears to come to a close. However, the orchestra play a simple two-chord movement back and forth, and the guitar figure is heard again, this time on synthesizer, while Joy Askew sings what are described in the sleeve notes as 'Madame Butterfly' vocals. Have a listen to Maria Callas's singing of this opera by Puccini (1858 – 1924) and you'll get the reference! The string section fades to nothing, the synthesiser motif is joined by guitar, becoming more urgent and four square, increasing in volume and suddenly we are plunged into...

## 'Acropolis Now' (4.21)

And now it's time for a heavy rock instrumental set, apparently, in a Greek restaurant. Of course. The title is a play on *Apocalypse Now*, the 1979 film by Francis Ford Coppola set in Vietnam and Cambodia. There is no hint of the Vietnam war here, although the heavy power chords which punctuate the introduction sound similar to a series of explosions. Or perhaps it's the sound of smashing dinner plates.

Following the powerful introduction, the joyful and rapid main melody is played on guitar and synth over a more restrained though still energetic backing with a prominent bass line adding to the sense of fun. To emphasise the Greek atmosphere the band throw in an amusing 'Hoy!' at the end of this section. This climax is unusually in a single bar of 3/4 time in contrast to all the traditional four-to-the-floor rockiness surrounding it. The initial melody is partially repeated before gathering steam over a syncopated rhythm which lands us back into the heavyweight introduction.

After a brief section of just bass and drums, a ghostly synthesiser solo takes centre stage, which is reminiscent of the keyboard introduction to 'The Gates of Babylon', the epic track on Rainbow's 1978 album *Long Live Rock'n'Roll*. Volume and intensity gradually increases throughout this section until a crescendo is reached, and a new melody begins at 3.15 on guitar.

This consists of four bars of 4/4 time followed by a single bar of 2/4, and then eight more bars of four over which a syncopated melody revolves, until the introduction is reprised once again. The music then collapses into a messy, improvised coda from which emerges the first theme again, with the final 'Hoy!' leading us straight into...

## 'Blaze Of Glory' (6.08)

...with Zummo's aggressively strummed acoustic guitar introduction. The title track compares the legacy of a classic rock musician (allusions to Elvis Presley are made, but the singer is never specifically referenced) who died young with the then-current 'wannabes'.

In the first verse Johnny, a young boy with 'a certain kind of look in his eye', is discovered and manipulated into becoming an artist with whom all the young boys ('being just dumb and restless') could now identify. The pre-chorus lines lay the ground for the rest of the tragedy; 'So tell me who'll take the blame for the way things turned out?'

Verse two is set six months later; Johnny is 'the biggest thing alive' and everyone is 'along for the ride'. However, the 'ride' starts to go too fast and Johnny just dies. Interestingly Jackson uses the word 'convenient' to describe the death. Possibly here he is considering the marketing and after-life long term sales potential of a star dying before his time. Bass and drums join the guitar for this verse, with the pre-chorus again adding to the sad tale; 'And he went up in flames, he did what he had to do'. For the chorus a slightly distorted electric guitar joins the mix; 'And they say it's a tragic story, he just wasn't there one day, but he went out in a blaze of glory and you and I, you and I just fade away'.

The third verse has the drums becoming more aggressive, and this is where Jackson turns his ire onto 'lots of guys like Johnny' who 'are all just cartoons, they all think they're Superman, but they can't even fly'. Jackson imagines Johnny's ghost walking around in Memphis ('when the moon is full and high',) and whether he sees 'these jokers' and his reaction; 'I wonder if he laughs or if he cries'.

The rest of the song is given over to a more heavily textured chorus, followed by an exquisite instrumental taken at half speed where the brass section plays a stirring melody which builds into a final chorus. Then there is a lengthy coda section where Jackson's repeated 'You and I just fade away's are interwoven with synth lines and melodies from the brass players. The music gradually itself fades away bringing side one, as it was, to a conclusion.

## 'Rant And Rave' (4.45)

The opening track of the second of the song cycles has more than a hint of Jethro Tull's 1969 hit 'Living In The Past' about it. The tempo, elements of the vocal melody, and the 5/4 time signature all place this music firmly in pseudo-prog rock territory. Then the brass players join in the action, Jackson gets stuck into the lyrics, and all trace of folkiness is swiftly banished. Written in the first person, this is a tirade of the highest order with Jackson taking on the character of a would-be terrorist ('I've got a bottle in my hand, I think I'll blow them up').

After two verses of this high energy angst the feel changes into a slower and sleazy sounding 4/4 time with a decidedly New York feel to it aided by the interjections from the saxophones and brass; 'Believe me you'll find out that everything's rotten from bottom to top through and through...'. The tension begins to build again and we're back to the original tempo and time signature for another angry verse before another collapse into the slower, secondary theme; 'Now who wants to be just a bug that they trample... instead of using the force of example now it's just the example of force'.

The music builds back to the first theme with a suitably spectacular and, at times, dissonant piano solo. A coda section of brass together with a rushing bass line against some manic drumming leads to the final chord and a seemingly improvised ending. This finally concludes with the drums setting up the steady 4/4 introductory rhythm for...

## 'Nineteen Forever' (5.48)

'Nineteen Forever' is another masterclass in pop-rock songwriting. Lyrically it's the eternal siren of the middle-aged not wanting to lose touch with their youth and past ambitions.

Musically the song is packed with melody, harmony, and a clever arrangement of the instruments, which belie the sometimes desperate-sounding nature of the words with an uplifting feel. Guitars and keyboards dominate with strong melodic lines, and Jackson's vocal delivery is crystal clear. Unusually the first verse ('Sometimes I feel so alive...') is not followed by a second, but an alternate chord progression ('I lose my fear of war and dying...'). This moves into a killer pre-chorus ('Wouldn't it be a drag to be like you? Settling down and having kids, and telling them what to do'), and finally a chorus. Here guitars chime, vocals harmonise, and the melodies remain top drawer.

The same structure is used again for the song's second section. There is a Who-based tip-of-the-hat in the pre-chorus; 'But I won't get fooled again'. After the second chorus, the bridge features more brass and another knowing nod, this time towards 'My Generation', with the line 'You know my dream's still alive... but I'm never going to be 35'. At the time of this record's release, Jackson was 35 years old.

The instrumental features a growly saxophone solo which is followed by repeated 'Nineteen Forever's, the song coming to an end with a sustained chord over which Jackson's character ironically shouts, 'One more time'. There is the sound of an audience cheering, drums and guitar punctuate the long organ chord and the sound fades away, as a mournful saxophone introduces the next song...

## 'The Best I Can Do' (3.10)

This is another slow ballad with a New York/*Night And Day* feel to it, highlighted by Morreale's emotive trumpet playing. Fretless bass is also prominent as a solo instrument amongst the sparkling piano accompaniment and Jackson's heavily reverberated vocals.

Whilst 'The Best I Can Do' is a 'beginning of a relationship' lyric, it is heavily weighted in the narrator's self-awareness with lines including 'I'll try to protect you, if I don't get too scared', 'I'll be right behind you, if you don't move too fast', and '...I'll never roam, not unless I have to'. After the second pair of short verses, Morreale has another superb solo reprising the vocal melody and the inherent resignation to Jackson's singing as he concludes it's 'the best I can do'. His 'best' is tempered by the knowledge of his past relationship history. There is a false ending at 3.06 before a final sustained phrase is joined by...

## 'Evil Empire' (3.45)

...strummed acoustic guitars, fretless bass and upbeat congas. This light and happy sounding feel is at odds with Jackson's lyrics; 'There's a country where no one knows what's going on in the rest of the world, there's a country where minds are closed, with just a few asking questions'.

Whilst the first verse may be directed at the former USSR and the Eastern Bloc ('You're either with or against us'), the second verse suggests the United States; 'There's a country that's great and wide, it's got the biggest of everything'. The next stanzas are particularly telling; 'You can't hide in a gunman's mask, or kill innocent folks and run, but if you're good at it they might ask, 'Come on over to the other side''. All of this is played out against a constantly cheerful, up-tempo arrangement of guitars and percussion.

The mood becomes stronger with the bridge section at 2.09; 'I could go on but what's the use, you can't fight them with songs. But think of this as just another tiny blow against the Empire, another blow against the Evil Empire'. At 2.30 the drums kick in and a lengthy, highly melodic acoustic guitar solo is heard amid repeats of the final words, the song coming to an end with a heavy left-hand lurch into electronica...

## 'Discipline' (5.01)

A drum machine, an alarm clock, a mechanised voice repeating 'You can't fight City Hall', strident brass, distorted guitar, and a cheesy sounding keyboard all form the basis of this song's introduction.

'Discipline', the song, is almost constantly resolute and unyielding; the concept itself can 'stop my hunger, quench my thirst, make me stronger, if it doesn't kill me first'. There's a lot going on in the mix underlining the intensity of the narrator's unspecified lifestyle, with no sense of space or relaxation until 2.38.

Here the sound pressure finally gives way to a section that again has a light jazz feel to it; 'But tonight I'm going to be my only slave, put on my CD of the sound of waves, and drift away until another day'. This respite is only brief as the opening texture and tempo soon return at 2.55. This continues with sound effects of taxis and various conversations over which the opening verse lines are repeated over and over again.

At 4.25, the song comes to an abrupt halt with 'Discipline can stop...'. The music is then heard as if being played in a room at the end of a long corridor, or down a phone line. This is overlaid with a slow piano melody as the relentless beat fades away.

## 'The Human Touch' (5.11)

The album's closing track is another of Jackson's magnificent ballads. The song is an appeal to an unspecified other to give and receive that all-important 'human touch' amongst the confusion and tensions of everyday life.

Piano, violin, and acoustic guitar feature in the introduction with the verse taking place over a backdrop of a heartbeat drum rhythm, and simple piano chords. The lyrics offer up contrasting views; sung in unison by Jackson and Askew 'Some say the world is spinning faster, some say it isn't fast enough, some people say they got the answer, and some are scared to say they can't keep up'. The pre-chorus grows in intensity and the chorus is another strongly melodic, involving affair, with an excellent counterpoint violin melody. An acoustic guitar melody brings the song back to a reprise of the introduction and a second verse, pre-chorus, and chorus.

At 2.44 there is a beautiful duet between violin and cello which grows to a crescendo before the dynamics die down again with just bass, drums and plucked violin playing in the bridge section. This has vague echoes of the hopeful atmosphere and musical texture of a slower version of 'Tomorrow's World'. Despite being 'nothing in the scheme of things, just microchips in big machines', Jackson's optimism remains strong that 'we can slow it down, and I know that I can make you see I'm on the side of you and me'. The music grows with increasing contributions from the vocalists building into the release of a reprise of the chorus at the original volume. A repeat of the introduction brings this highly satisfying song to a peaceful, positive conclusion.

# Laughter & Lust

Personnel:
Joe Jackson: vocals, keyboards
Graham Maby: bass, vocals
Joy Askew: vocals, keyboards
Tom Teeley: guitar, vocals
Sue Hadjopoulos: percussion, drums
Dan Hickey: drums
Michael Morreale: trumpet
Tony Aiello: saxophones
Annie Whitehead: trombone
Charles McCracken: cello
Written by Joe Jackson, except where noted
Produced by Joe Jackson and Ed Roynesdal
Engineered by Larry Alexander
Recorded at Dreamland Studio, Woodstock, New York
Assisted by Dave Cook and John Yates
Mixed at Electric Ladyland, New York City
Assisted by Adam Yellin
Released: April 1991 on Virgin Records
Highest chart position UK: 41, USA: 116

Despite a substantial tour, *Blaze of Glory* was a relative disappointment commercially, partially due to a perceived lack of support from A&M. Shortly after its release Jackson left the record company. And, as surely as night follows day (sorry), A&M released a compilation album, *Steppin' Out; The Very Best of Joe Jackson* which became a top ten hit in the United Kingdom.

Jackson's first album for his new record label, Virgin, was preceded by a five-week United States tour between September and October 1990. Billed as 'Joe Jackson's Workshop', it included performances of songs to be recorded for the new album as a way of testing fresh material before a live audience. A&M were mistaken with thename for their retrospective album; the title should have included the words 'So Far', as *Laughter & Lust* is right up there with Jackson's very best work.

In an interview in 1994 with *Cash Box*, the songwriter said:

*Laughter & Lust*, I felt, was the closest thing I could possibly do to a commercial pop record that I thought everyone was gonna love. And it was not very successful in the States. It did okay in Europe, actually. So, it wasn't a complete flop.

*Laughter & Lust* is a great collection of songs with a crystal clear, fresh and lively sounding production that loses the then-fashionable 'bells and whistles' studio excesses which were allowed sonic space on *Blaze Of Glory*. The energy level is as high as the sound is bright; there's only space for two ballads and these are both in the second half of what was Side Two. The emphasis of the album is on highly melodic, straightforward pop-rock songs to which Jackson's trademark vocals and clever, thought-provoking lyrics add layers of depth and class.

## 'Obvious Song' (4.13)

Opening with a gradually increasing crescendo of discordant instrumental noise, a lively piano riff kicks off 'Obvious Song', which is soon joined by the rest of the band at an urgent tempo. Jackson turns on the vitriol for this attack on the hypocrisy of the 'haves' when confronted with the 'have nots'.

This is illustrated in the first verse, where a 'man in the jungle' who is about to cut down a tree just to 'make ends meet' is confronted by a 'rock'n'roll millionaire from the USA' who wants him to spare the tree because 'we gotta save this world – starting with your land'. Jackson is quick to point out that the American does 'three to the gallon in his big white car'; someone who sings until 'he polluted the air'. Brass joins in for the rousing chorus; 'And the stars are looking down through a hole in the sky. And if they can see they cry – that's obvious'. This is followed by an allusion to the fall of the Berlin Wall in 1989; 'The walls are coming down between the West and East, you don't have to be a hippie to believe in peace – that's obvious'.

For the second verse, the focus transfers to a drug dealer 'selling crack to get by' who is arrested. Jackson sees the kid as 'another foot soldier in a stupid little war', someone who is caught between 'the supplier only dreaming of money, and the demand of the man with money who needs a little help to dream'. The chorus contains the memorable couplet, 'So we starve all the teachers and recruit more marines, how come we don't even know what that means? It's obvious'.

The instrumental section (2.46-3.12) brings the brass players to the fore with a simple anthemic melody which climbs, reaching a peak where a single, distorted guitar phrase takes over. Teeley skilfully controls his sustained final note as it moves into feedback, adding a slight modulation to the note with the vibrato arm , which increases the lively, exciting sound that Jackson and Roynesdal were intent on capturing.

The introduction is then repeated and we are into the coda section. This is where this otherwise excellent and powerful opener starts to meander as it consists of repeated excerpts from the chorus, with Askew contributing strong complementary vocals. The song concludes on a held chord with just a hint of guitar feedback. As a statement of intent for the rest of the album, however, 'Obvious Song' sets out its stall immediately. Listeners are in for a highly melodic, rocking, and intellectually engaging ride. There's little time to draw breath as we're...

## 'Goin' Downtown' (3.05) (Jackson/Barfield)

A very rare compositional collaboration, 'Goin' Downtown' was written with another former A&M signing, Drew Barfield. It isn't clear which parts of the number are Jackson and which Barfield, as it comes across as a fully-fledged Jackson composition, packed with melodic ideas and lyrical barbs.

The song sounds like it could have found a home on either *Look Sharp!* or *I'm The Man*. Jackson sings in the first person about his choices for an evening; 'I could cool out, I could hang loose, I could lay my head back in this comfortable noose. I could watch the paint dry on these rented walls, or I could run wild with the first wild thing who calls'.

This is set against a medium tempo and is fundamentally a blues shuffle, where again, the brass play a prominent role, especially with their triplet based melody introduction. Piano and drums power the syncopated groove along and 'Goin' Downtown' is soon into its harmonised chorus where people 'stand round and stare, and put people down for not being there'.

The second verse turns to someone laughing at a girl having fun; 'To show some emotion just isn't done'. Jackson wryly observes that in this place someone is 'only as good as the cut of your clothes'. A second chorus leads into a manic, distorted guitar solo over the verse's chord progression. After a repeat of the second chorus, Jackson says 'There's got to be more to life than this', and the song moves into its coda section with repeats of the title words and general instrumental busyness. The opening brass flurry brings things to a sudden conclusion.

'Goin' Downtown' is a decent enough song but, finding itself sandwiched between two great ones shows it to be more filling than thrilling.

## 'Stranger Than Fiction' (3.40)

Now, this is much more like it. 'Stranger Than Fiction' is a riot of colour and joy, powered along by infectious chord progressions, stellar melodies, and involving lyrics.

Opening with a sing-a-long 'na na na' vocal melody, Jackson's expressive vocals are interspersed with some great clean guitar work by Teeley, occasional lush vocal harmonies, and a great groove from the drums and percussion. The chorus is as memorable as it is melodic, and the entire song has a fantastic spirit about it. Set in an appropriate major key the song is wry, uplifting, and optimistic. Unsurprisingly 'Stranger Than Fiction' was the first single to be released from the album.

Structurally it's straightforward (introduction, verse, chorus, (repeat), bridge, short organ solo over the verse chord sequence, chorus and coda), but within the relative constrictions of the 'pop' format, Jackson allows his talents full rein.

The best lyrics are found in the bridge section; 'I know that sometimes love goes, but sometimes it comes back to get you. And when love grows, it grows like a flower or grows like a tumour, love shows that God has a sense of humour'. Simultaneously wisecracking and vulnerable, Jackson also hits the spot with his comments on life referenced in the chorus, seeing it as filled with 'disasters and friction', 'bizarre contradictions', and 'ever immune to prediction' but no matter how weird life may be 'only love can be stranger than fiction'.

## 'Oh Well' (2.29) (Green)

One of Peter Green's classic songs for the original blues version of Fleetwood Mac (released in 1969 on the album *Then Play On*) is given a muscular workout. Putting aside all of *Jumpin' Jive* this is the first time a cover version has featured on a Joe Jackson studio album. 'Oh Well' is, and always will be, a great song, but why is it included here? It's not as if Jackson lacks any ability as a songwriter.

So what's the idea then? The vocal lines suit Jackson's voice well, and the band sound like they are having a blast playing the music, but fundamentally this is just a cover version; a very good one, but nothing more. Aside from a rockier, slightly faster interpretation with enhanced instrumentation (especially in the percussion department), over and above the slinky blues rock of the original, this is otherwise just a faithful and accurate rendition of a familiar song. Puzzling.

## 'Jamie G' (2.03)

A bright, piano introduction supported by a rapid, syncopated drum rhythm underpins this brisk, Cuban influenced pop song which brings us back to the world of relationships. Bristling with lively percussion, high-pitched and busy keyboard playing, and a catchy chorus, 'Jamie G' has a carnival air about it, which is lifted still further by a modulation from A major to Bb major for the final chorus. Intriguingly it is not clear whether Jamie is male or female. Does it matter? The song comes to what sounds like a false ending, and after a brief pause, the drums begin again at the same tempo, but this slows and changes into the introduction for...

## 'Hit Single' (3.35)

This is a fun song with a sarcastic edge where Jackson takes on the persona of a vinyl record, the titular 'hit single'. Written in the first person, the singing seven inch sounds like a 'man about town'; 'I've got a line or two that never fails, and every time you look around I'll be there on your tail'. Jackson views hit singles as 'nothing special' but they get 'right beneath your skin'.

The bridge, which merges smoothly into the final verse, hits the lyrical nail firmly on the head: The single dies and arrives in 'pure pop heaven' where the angels gather around. They 'ask me for my whole life story and ask for that fabulous sound'. As the third verse commences the commercial realities of the music business are brought into sharp focus; 'But I know they're gonna stop me, as I start going through every line, and say 'Please, not the whole damn album, nobody has that much time, please, just the hit single''.

Musically this number has pastiche written right through it. Cheesy organ, a syncopated 4/4-time drum rhythm (reminiscent of several 1960s chart-toppers), chiming guitars, and a catchy chorus with excellent backing vocals all contribute to the mocking and yet celebratory sounding atmosphere. There is a lower octave piano instrumental, and the closing section, after repeated 'You gotta love that Number One's, has a beautifully phrased, modulation laden, and vaguely familiar-sounding jazz guitar coda.

## 'It's All Too Much' (4.20)

We're back to guitar-dominated, driving rock in this ode to the problems of an over-laden consumerist society, and how much harder this is to bear when alone. 'It's All Too Much' is a great, fast-paced slice of pop, simultaneously slick and sharp, packed full of great melodies and perceptive lyrics. Chiming guitars and vigorous percussion are the backbone to the wordiest song in this collection, the verses and chorus frequently modulating between E major and G major.

Jackson's commentary on consumer choice and the effect too much has on one person has many highlights, with several great stanzas; 'I hate this supermarket, but I have to say it makes me think, a hundred mineral waters, fun to guess which ones are safe to drink', and 'What shall we do this evening, send out for some sushi and champagne? Stay in and watch TV, 50 channels can't all be the same'. The post-chorus section lays bare the narrator's chief issue; 'It's all too much for me to stand, so much supply and no demand, there's just too much for me to do, especially without you ... won't you please come home?'

The album's clear-sounding production really lifts 'It's All Too Much'. All the instruments are spaciously recorded, dynamic changes and new textures shine through effortlessly, and the track sparkles with energy and life, despite the ultimately downbeat lyrics. The chorus is outstanding, the pace never lets up, and the song is performed with terrific spirit and attack, finally coming to rest over a sustained guitar chord and some dissipating bongos.

## 'When You're Not Around' (4.00)

'When You're Not Around' retains the guitars and percussion of 'It's All Too Much' against a solid rock drum backing. This is another melody and harmony saturated track which alternates between driving 'new wave' sections and more reflective, reggae-influenced pre-chorus parts.

Like a lot of great pop songs, 'When You're Not Around' is straightforward in structure, relying on a revolving guitar riff and a constant, steady tempo. The first-person lyrics centre around someone experiencing intense feelings for an unnamed other, as witnessed in the magnificent chorus where the vocal melody and harmonies just soar; 'And if I didn't feel so high, and if I didn't feel so proud, then I wouldn't cry, I wouldn't feel so down, when you're not around'.

'When You're Not Around' is another sharp, snappy and catchy pop-rock song with a terrific groove. Unusually for such a guitar-driven track, it features one of Jackson's instantly identifiable octave piano solos as a short instrumental section after the second chorus. The backing vocals really pile on for the repeat of the chorus, and Teeley has a gorgeous, Beatles-esque arpeggio sequence under which the track gradually fades.

## 'The Other Me' (4.11)

A song of regret and indecision, 'The Other Me' is a slower-paced track over-laden with melody and harmony, dynamics, textural changes, and a great lyric. Here's a person caught between being attracted to another whilst already being in a long-term relationship. As with 'Jamie G', the sex of the narrator is left to the listener's mind; 'When I see you there alone, it almost breaks my heart, but it doesn't break enough for me to break my whole life apart'.

The verse is dominated by violins, piano and percussion, with occasional strands of guitar drifting in and out. The pre-chorus changes the feel with arpeggiated guitar and busier percussion, whilst the chorus is decorated with unison vocals, rising to a climax with distorted guitar and syncopated drums attacking the emotive chorus. The only dubious lyric in this otherwise fantastic section is the rhyming of 'The other me would stay all night, the other me would hold you tight'. Luckily the power of the underlying music smoothes over this 'sixth form' level poetry.

After the second chorus, the bridge is another absolute belter with gorgeous vocal harmonies, and a harmonic tension building into a reprise of the chorus. Listen out for the extended 'whoh-whoh' vocal link between the two sections at 3.19 as Jackson encapsulates the exaltation and frustration of his situation. The song slows slightly to a gentler end and is four minutes of pop perfection, worthy of a place on anybody's playlist.

## 'Trying To Cry' (6.34)

The album's first true ballad changes the mood entirely. A single, sustained electric guitar chord is joined by reflective percussion and Jackson's reverberated vocals. There is a hypnotic quality to the simple underlying harmonic progression, and the spacious style of production which gives the track a dream-like quality. The first four minutes of the album's longest song feature just two chords, a G major (add2) and E minor 7.

This suits the introspective lyrics as Jackson observes a 'guy in the corner', drinking and smoking, at an emotional low point. Jackson expands on the unnamed individual; 'I've seen it in the mirror, and I've seen it in my friends, when we realise we've lost ourselves and we try to make amends'. Despite the man's inner turmoil, his childhood conditioning prevents him from doing what he so desperately needs to do – cry. This is emphasised in the chorus; 'Remember what your brother said, remember what your brother said, "'I'll tell the whole class if I see you"'", and 'Remember what your mother said, remember what your mother said "'Never be a man if you do"'. These lines are sung by a low-pitched female voice, with Jackson joining in with the repeated 'Now he's trying to cry...'.

After the second chorus, a ghostly string synth chord progression grows and grows until breaking like the bank of a dam at 4.43. This and the following eight bars have an epic 'Pink Floyd-ian' quality to them, which gradually diminishes as a higher-pitched female voice repeatedly intones 'It's alright'. The opening music returns, and the melody for 'Never be a man if you do' is heard again, this time played on muted trumpets and placed well back in the mix. The music fades leaving just the highly atmospheric percussion, which slowly disappears.

## 'My House' (4.26)

Agitation, frustration, anger, bitterness, suppressed temper; all are present and correct in this tense little number. The piano, percussion, and rim-shot drums introduction fade in as Jackson's taut vocal tone conveys a character in a situation a lot of people can relate to; 'I'm moving my car forward a foot at a time, another red light, another warning sign. Tapping my fingers to the radio, but I don't hear a thing. Watching the hookers move in and out of the light, one of these days, one of these days...'

The song explodes with drums and distorted guitar in the pre-chorus; 'One of these days, I'm gonna smash somebody's car, and smash the copper's face as they take me away'. The chorus, 'But I gotta go home now' with the backing refrain of 'Don't want to go to my house', is played out over the verse chord sequence.

For the second verse, the mood deepens further with another killer line encapsulating adult life; 'Me and Suzy used to read the news and stay up all night. We used to see a lot of people, then we just got tired, and gave birth to a perfect little alibi'. After the second chorus, the song enters its coda section with verse lyrics dotted around the revolving piano ostinato and Jackson intoning 'one of these days, one of these days' as the rest of the instrumentation fades away, leaving just the piano coming to an eventual end.

## 'The Old Songs' (3.32)

The mood shifts again. Opening with a cheesy sounding, slightly detuned piano, the drums kick in with a strummed acoustic guitar in a swaying 6/8 time. Despite its major key setting Jackson unleashes his bile on 'another happy couple on the road to emptiness. I think of my father and mother, can they imagine how two people can get in this mess?'

The chorus is another melodic micro-masterpiece with an uplifting tune against which, again, words tell a different story; 'But the old songs say love's forever, and the old songs never say die. But a song can't keep us together; how can that beautiful song be a lie?' Jackson holds the 'old songs' responsible for 'filling hearts with rebellion and romance'.

The second verse and chorus offer no respite; 'Play us another one, play us all the hopes and dreams of twenty years ago'. These songs are 'all over the bloody radio, it's like they're telling us there's nowhere left to go'. In the chorus Jackson references 'Be My Baby' (The Ronettes, 1963) and 'She Loves You' (The Beatles, 1964), and underlines their staying power with the climactic line; 'I like those songs, but I'd like something new'. The bitterness is not far away as 'all our great expectations turn to alimony and remorse'.

At 2.46, a new chord sequence ushers in an instrumental coda section with backing vocals 'la la la'-ing over an acoustic guitar and subtle piano fills which conclude the song. It's an unusual end to an impassioned composition.

## 'Drowning' (5.09)

In a similar vein to the end of *Blaze Of Glory*, *Laughter & Lust's* final track is another piano ballad, this one, however, being singularly dispiriting in its lyric; 'I don't love you, but I'm lost. Thinking of you, and the ghosts of so many special moments that passed so quickly at the time'.

A strong contribution from the cello and subtle electric guitar fills out a texture where percussion and drums are absent. Matching the lyrical metaphor the music doesn't adhere to a strict tempo, it moves back and forth, wavelike, pulling and pushing gently, rarely staying in a regular pulse for any significant length of time. Jackson's vocals feel incredibly personal here, a missive to a failing or failed relationship, although, again, the respective sexes of the participants are omitted; 'I don't need you, but it's so hard to be without you. You batter my defences down, but so gently, like some sweet hypnosis and the world just slips away...'

Following the second verse, there is a six-note descending chromatic vocal melody supported by a sliding chord sequence where the acoustic guitar becomes mandolin-like. After a short pause, the music gathers itself again for its final verse; 'It's dark, my heart is pounding, I'm sinking down into a pool of passion, there's laughter as I drown'. There is a brief moment of optimism; 'And then I look into your eyes, and something melts, I shake inside and cool water washes me all over...'. but this is soon dashed with '...washes me away, and still I'm drowning'.

The instrumental is repeated, eleven steps this time, descending still further into the musical depths as reverb is added to Jackson's voice, and the music disappears to be replaced by the sound of waves on a shore. After so much uplifting material, 'Drowning' is a despondent epitaph, its mood acting as a prelude to the intimate atmosphere Jackson would create with his next album.

# Night Music

Personnel:
Joe Jackson: piano, electric piano, organ, synthesisers and samplers, celeste, accordion, tom-toms, bells, vibes, cymbals, Salvation Army drum, computer sequencing.
Guest musicians:
Mary Rowell: viola ('Nocturne No.1', 'The Man Who Wrote Danny Boy', 'Only The Future', 'Nocturne No.4') and violin ('Nocturne No.4')
Jean Laurence: ondes martenot ('Nocturne No.1', and 'Sea Of Secrets')
Taylor Carpenter: vocals ('Ever After')
Michael Morreale: trumpet ('Ever After')
Gary Burke: drums ('Ever After')
Maier Brennan: vocals ('The Man Who Wrote Danny Boy')
Dick Morgan: oboe ('Nocturne No.3' and 'Sea Of Secrets')
Renee Fleming: vocals ('Lullaby')
Albert Regna: clarinet and bass clarinet ('Lullaby')
Graham Maby: bass ('Only The Future')
Tony Aiello: flute ('Only The Future')
Mary Wooten: cello ('Nocturne No.4')
Ed Roynesdal: programming and sampling
Written and arranged by Joe Jackson
Produced by Joe Jackson and Ed Roynesdal
Recorded at The Hit Factory, New York, and at Jacobs, Surrey, England
Engineers: Andy Grassy, Ken Thomas, Carl Glanville, and Ed Roynesdal
Production coordinator: Tony Unger
Technical support: Rob Deck, Benjamin Austin, Paul Meehan
Digital editing and compilation by Charles Habit at Sony Classical, New York
Mastered by Ted Jensen at Sterling Sound, New York
Released: October 1994 on Virgin Records
Highest chart positions: Did not chart

Three years passed between *Laughter & Lust* and *Night Music*. During this time Jackson wrote music for two films (*I'm Your Man* – 1992 and *Three Of Hearts* – 1993) but no soundtrack albums were made available.

Whatever fans were expecting after the guitar orientated, mainstream pop-rock of *Blaze Of Glory* and *Laughter & Lust, Night Music* probably wasn't it. Best listened to on headphones for a totally embracing experience, or in darkness on a high-quality hi-fi system, *Night Music* is another unexpected diversion in Jackson's musical road trip. It is a subdued fusion of pop and classical styles which creates a unique atmosphere that rewards repeated listenings.

Writing on his website, Jackson explained the rationale behind the album:

I was coming out of both touring burnout and writer's block when I made this. I started to think that musically everyone was trying to out-do each other in being harsh and aggressive and kind of bashing you over the head, and I wanted to go against the grain and make something gentle, dreamlike, and beautiful. Someone once told me they liked to fall asleep listening to it, and I took it as a compliment.

**In an interview with the *Montreal Gazette* in April 1995 he said of the album:**

I wanted to make something that was beautiful. […] I wanted to suggest a nocturnal, quiet, reflective mood, but I also wanted to suggest the magic of dreams. The logic of dreams, which is different to the logic of being awake. A non-linear logic. I think a lot of this record makes perfect sense, but in a dream-like way.

## 'Nocturne No 1' (4.00)

'Nocturne No.1' sets the album's overall tone with a slow tempo, languid sustained melodies, and an introspective atmosphere. The counterpoint between the keyboards and viola is enticing, with rises and falls in dynamics, and unusual jazz-influenced harmonies featuring strongly in the first section (0.00-2.12), with a descending melody duet between keyboards and viola leading into a pensive section which fades.

The second half is initially sparser with a two-note repeated bass line. Sustained notes from the viola and occasional interjections from vibraphones are heard behind a pulsing lower range keyboard melody which increases in pitch, tempo, and volume to a dramatic pause. The first themes are reprised at a slower tempo. The concluding music is played on piano with sustained strings lending an air of mystery.

## 'Flying' (2.46)

Jackson's first vocal appearance is initially 'a cappella'. It's a great lyric and melody; 'The older I get the more stupid I feel... I don't know what's going on'. The vocal melody is shared around the backing instruments with syncopated piano, and synths prominent in the mix. The first verse concludes with 'Tired of trying to be strong when I should be crying', as the music slows to a pause.

The piano re-establishes itself for the second verse ('The further I go the less distance I see, leave behind another home') with Jackson moving into falsetto towards the end of the next, possibly autobiographical couplet; 'The harder I try the less people I please'. Strings take over the melodic role in a short instrumental section before the third verse; 'The older I get the more lucid I feel, let it go and let it come, tired of trying to belong when I could be flying'.

'Flying' is an unusual song; it never feels settled musically, and this is presumably deliberate, mirroring the simultaneous clarity and frustration of the words. The occasional brief silences in the song (0.41 and 2.20) are devoid of any reverberation. Consequently, the music, and this applies across the majority of the album, sounds very 'close', as if Jackson is performing in the same room as the listener. It's a very different style of production.

## 'Ever After' (4.40)

Opening with a *Body and Soul* style, anthemic sounding trumpet solo over the sustained organ, a reggae rhythm is quickly established on synth. Jackson's lyrics are set at the end of a relationship; 'Now that you're gone, nothing is wrong but everything's changed. Words in your hand, do I set them in stone or throw them away? Now everything we did, like photographs that always moved and that wasn't strange. Now they're in the can, let's put them on a shelf. Let's put them in the ground they'll never move again'.

Harmony vocals join for the chorus and numerous 'ever after's bounce around the stereo mix with a subtle trumpet in the background. A second verse and chorus are followed by a more optimistic tone... 'It'll be alright'.

This new section (2.42-3.28) builds in texture with drums providing an explosive backing to the simple keyboard riff, which crescendoes and then relaxes both in volume and tension. The synth reggae sequence reappears over which Jackson sings a wordless 'Barbershop' style melody against himself. The backing music fades, leaving just this choral-esque section which in turn disappears.

'Ever After' feels more like a 'traditional' Jackson song, if such a thing exists. If it belongs on any other Jackson album *Night And Day* or *Body And Soul* are possible homes, although if performed live with a typical rock band backing, it wouldn't sound out of place on either *Look Sharp!* or *I'm The Man*. Lyrically and melodically strong and memorable, there is a constant pulse, rises and falls in vocal and musical tension, and an intriguing mixture of instruments which, on paper, don't look like they'll work together. On disc they absolutely do.

## 'Nocturne No 2' (4.07)

This opens with a strident piano two-note figure which is developed as it descends in pitch, immediately re-establishing a new, darker mood with bass and synth in subtle support. The music quietens and gains a more pastoral feel with its slow, sustained melody synth lines and harmonic interplay.

Gradually elements of tension are introduced as the volume slowly grows and falls, rising again to a climax at 2.28, where an arpeggio figure on synth has an overlaid piano melody borrowed from the opening theme. The pastoral style returns at 3.05 and expands until, at 3.37, a more hopeful tone is briefly struck with a new tempo. The first piano figure reappears before the music slows and ends.

Elements of 'Nocturne No 2' have an early Mike Oldfield feel to them, especially in the quieter, more melodic passages. Jackson's distinctive piano style and the carefully structured use of dynamics, however, ensure that such comparisons (and they are meant to be complimentary) are fleeting. 'Nocturne

No 2' is another example of Jackson creating a micro-musical world all its own, at times mysterious and unsettling, elsewhere calming and restorative.

## 'The Man Who Wrote 'Danny Boy'' (5.18)

This is the best track on the album, 'The Man Who Wrote 'Danny Boy'' is a clever re-imagining of the Faustian legend; a man making a pact with the Devil; his soul in exchange for, in this case, musical success and consequent fame.

The 'Danny Boy' of the title is, of course, the famous ballad written by the English songwriter Frederic Wetherly in 1913, which he adapted from the traditional Irish tune, 'Londonderry Air'. It is this genre which dominates Jackson's song; there is a lilting 3/4 time signature, a Celtic influenced vocal melody, and viola and harp feature as the main accompaniment,

For Jackson's character in this song (which may be autobiographical) his dream is 'to live for all time in some perfect refrain like the man who wrote 'Danny Boy''. Unhappy with the quality of the work he has produced so far, he welcomes the appearance of the Devil in his studio room at 'three in the morning' who offers him a deal; 'Blow away all your struggles and take your soul for a toy'.

At this, the gentle mood changes, becoming more dramatic, and quicker with heavy piano and timpani joining the soundscape; 'And I said if you're real then I'll ask you a question, while most of us turn into ashes or dust, just you and that other guy go on forever, but who writes the history and who do I trust?'. The music slows and quietens back to its original style as the Devil charms the innocent, claiming how he finds it amusing that all human artistic endeavour goes 'on to tape, on to paper, or into the air', all to become 'lost and forgotten outside of his kind employ'.

The music rises again into a reprise of the dramatic mood as Jackson imagines he can hear 'a great sound in the distance, of whiskey-soaked singing and laughter and cheers, and they're saying that song could bring tears to a glass eye, so pass me the papers I'll sign them in blood'. Just as 'the smell of brimstone was turned into greasepaint' and the crowd's roar like the 'furies of hell', the narrator hears the applause and the sound of 'bells ringing', only to be dragged back to reality by 'the sound of a woman's voice from the next room'.

The appearance of Clannad vocalist Maire Brennan's soft Irish voice at this point is stunning; 'Come to me now, come lay down beside me, whatever you're doing you're too gone to see, you can't hold onto shadows no more than to years, so be glad for the pleasures we're young enough to enjoy'.

Left to his own devices Jackson ponders what has happened; '...maybe we're all living inside a dream'. But his ambition remains undimmed; 'You can say what you like, when I'm gone then you'll see, I'll be down in the dark, down underground, with Shakespeare and Bach and the man who wrote 'Danny Boy''. The music doesn't resolve, ending instead on a long, beautifully phrased viola solo and a single chord leaving the listener to wonder what might happen in the future...

# 'Nocturne No 3' (4.28)

A slow and at times achingly beautiful piece of music, 'Nocturne No 3', is initially, to this listener, a perfect encapsulation of a quiet, ink-black sky, filled with stars. Set against a slow keyboard arpeggio, a soothing, hypnotic mood is quickly established with a simple descending piano melody. A clarinet develops this with another harmony clarinet part joining the texture completing the first section.

The initial keyboard theme is then repeated an octave higher whilst the clarinets stay at their original pitch. Sustained synthesiser chords in the background add sonic support. Against the background of repeated keyboard arpeggios, a disquieting change of mood occurs at 1.43, where the sound of a radio being tuned is brought into earshot, with some fairground organ style harmonies adding to the aural confusion. An oboe rescues the tune amidst this interference with occasional short sforzando interjections from the other instruments.

At 2.36, a slightly dissonant electric piano melody takes the place of the oboe, and then the higher octave piano phrases are heard sparsely amongst slight orchestral crescendos. This inherent tension gently builds until the clarinets reappear at 3.24, adding a measure of calm. By the four-minute mark the instruments play less and less, leaving the three-note keyboard arpeggio decorated with a high pitched electric piano melody, which drifts into nothing.

# 'Lullaby' (6.20)

Initially an almost direct continuation of mood established throughout much of 'Nocturne No 3', 'Lullaby' maintains the dream-like piano atmosphere to which is added a ghostly, quasi-operatic vocal performance from Renee Fleming. This brings a sense of disquiet over the gently relentless minor key arpeggios. The melodies and dynamics gently rise and fall until, at 2.02, Jackson's processed vocal enters the picture; 'Shall I stay or go through the door? Will the pen to flow? Watch the stars, sleep's a chore'. The only backing to this is the piano with a single church bell strike, and a soft bass distant in the soundscape.

The mood changes dramatically at 2.45 into what becomes the centrepiece of the composition. The tempo increases, a synth chord crescendoes into a descending electric piano melody, and an oboe provides an unsettling melody until Jackson's next superb lyrics. These are set against a discordant backdrop which, unusually, includes an accordion in the mixture; 'The moon is growing cold, it hangs like a sliver of tin. How do our dreams unfold? And why are my bones feeling thin?' The tension increases further into a climax of a descending chord sequence with the oboe flowing in and out of the texture together with synthesisers and piano; 'I watch my pen as though my fingers could shatter like icicles and before my eyes lie glittering and useless on a field of snow'.

At this point (4.24) the opening theme is reprised in its entirety with Fleming's sustained phrases resetting the lonely nighttime mood. The music comes to an end with a slowing of the arpeggiated piano pattern.

'Lullaby' is hypnotic and disquieting. Like other tracks on *Night Music* it is not a composition designed for easy consumption. There are layers of instrumentation used in the creation of its diverse moods, and a memorable lyric which is as evocative as it is unsettling.

## 'Only The Future' (4.55)

A much more optimistic and hopeful tone is struck, musically at least, with the combination of a flute melody over a briskly strummed acoustic guitar synthesised sound. This is given greater weight by the addition of saxophone and some pulsating percussion in the background. The chorus motif is heard, then the opening theme is repeated with the viola joining in and adding sonic colour.

Jackson's vocals appear over the guitar and percussion backing at 1.40, but the lyrics do not match the music's positive tone; 'Something's coming, something big, something I can't stand. Dark as the ocean, secret and cruel, something I can't command. Something's waiting, down a mugger's alley, to see what's on my mind. Take a deep breath, start walking faster, it's dark, but I'm not blind'. The mood only becomes more hopeful with the verse's final words as the melody and chord structure changes; 'You never know, if you push at this wall, my hand could pass through. So, this cloud of unknowing could disappear too'. Harmony vocals join for the title words.

A brief discordant section follows (2.51-3.27) where Maby's busy bass lines are heard way back in the mix, until the opening theme is reprised, this time with greater strength. The blend of flute and viola are particularly effective here, with the ever-present, active percussion driving the music along. This instrumental section comes to a sudden end after some melodic flourishes, with the isolated keyboards playing a slower version of the 'Only The Future' melody and chords.

## 'Nocturne No 4' (6.12)

The opening motif of 'Nocturne No 4' is a reduction of the 'Only The Future' melody to two notes, and is heard here with different instrumentation as a brief 'introduction to the introduction'.

Seventeen seconds in and a rolling arpeggio figure on keyboards and cello provide the actual beginning to the album's longest track. A gentle, high pitched melody is added on synthesiser and developed until 1.50, when a new mood appears. This is faster and is based around a strict quaver rhythm in the accompaniment, with the melody transferred to the violin and viola. This slows into a beautiful solo violin passage before the opening theme is reprised (2.40-3.25) and once again, the string melody is replayed over the brisker tempo.

This tune passes briefly through several keys before coming to another section of solo playing (4.27-5.00). The first theme is played again with the violins moving into the accompaniment; at 5.31, sustained chords and fragments of piano leave a sense of unease to a coda section of what has otherwise been a relaxing, hypnotic piece of music.

## 'Sea Of Secrets' (5.25)

Opening with a flurry of electric piano arpeggios immediately sets the watery scene. A strong oboe melody, slow and stately, is added to the wavelike chordal flow, which slows prior to Jackson's vocal entry; 'I'm sinking into a sea of secrets, warm and green, down and down back to times and places never seen'. His voice is treated with plenty of reverberation to add to the atmosphere. The chorus is powerfully melodic, briefly sung in falsetto; 'Now and then, I can wake and I remember, just one secret thing, through the rain I can keep a candle burning under the skin of the world'.

The introduction is reprised before a second verse; 'It's sinking in, no need for fear of drowning, drift away. These monsters here are only faces I don't wear by day'. This is followed by another chorus section; 'Now and then I can wake, and in the mirror, demons turn to friends. Through the pain, I can dig a little deeper under the skin of the world'.

At 4.00, the melody from 'Nocturne No 1' is played at a much slower pace over the electric piano arpeggios, the music descending lower and lower, losing speed, and finally coming to rest on a very long final major chord.

'Sea Of Secrets' is another surprising song in this involving collection. Highly atmospheric, mysterious, and not a little unsettling, it shows Jackson writing exactly what he wants to write and hoping his fan base will follow him as he continues his unique musical journey.

# Heaven & Hell

Personnel:

Joe Jackson: piano, electric piano, organ, clavinet, synthesiser, samples, percussion and drum loops, vocals ('Fugue 1: More Is More', 'Passacaglia: A Bud And A Slice', 'Fugue 2: Song Of Daedalus'), voice of 'Soul In Torment' ('Angel'), voices of 'Cynicism' and 'Greed': ('Tuzla')

Nadja Salerno-Sonnerberg: solo violin ('Prelude' and 'Fugue 2: Song Of Daedalus'

Dawn Upshaw: voice of Angel ('Angel') and Voice of Forgetfulness ('Tuzla')

Suzanne Vega: vocal of Fallen Angel ('Angel')

Mary Rowell: violin ('Angel')

Allison Cornell: viola ('Angel')

Sue Hadjopoulos: congas and bongos ('Angel' and 'The Bridge')

Joy Askew: voice of Conscience ('Tuzla')

Brad Roberts: vocals ('Passacaglia: A Bud And A Slice')

Judith LeClair: bassoon ('Passacaglia: A Bud And A Slice')

Dan Hickey: drums ('Right')

Kenny Aronoff: drums ('Right')

Jared Crawford: plastic buckets in Times Square

Jane Silberry: vocals ('The Bridge')

Laura Seaton, Sandra Park, Joyce Hammann, Todd Reynolds, Mark Feldman, Naomi Katz, Cenovia Cummins, James Tsao: violins

Juliet Haffner, Allison Cornell, David Blinn, Katherine Beeson, Mary Rowell: Violas

Eric Friedlander, Stephanie Cummins, Richard Locker: cellos

William Sloat: acoustic bass

All music, words and arrangements by Joe Jackson

Produced by Joe Jackson and Ed Roynesdal

Engineered by Dan Gellert

Recorded at Avatar, New York City, Winter 1996/1997

Assisted by Rich Alvy

Mastered by Ted Jensen at Sterling Sound, New York City

Released: September 1997 on Sony Classical

Highest chart positions: did not chart

Breaking the 'W.T.F-ometer' with an impressive score of eleven, Jackson's next album was like nothing his fans had heard before. Dark, intense, atmospheric, disturbing and powerful; *Heaven & Hell* is all of these, and more. A concept album which presents seven songs, where each one deals with one of the 'Deadly Sins', is certainly ambitious. Inevitably Jackson pulls it off, producing a collection that takes time and patience to appreciate, but is well worth the effort. Never an album to be filed under 'easy listening' in record stores it's tempting to think that *Heaven & Hell* will be 'hard work'. Repeated plays bring forth a dark humour, unusual instrumental arrangements, and strong compositions. However, the eight tracks are not conventionally structured and they take time to establish themselves in the mind.

Billed as 'Joe Jackson & Friends', the majority of the heavy lifting is undertaken by Jackson himself, supported by sterling contributions from the string players, guest vocalists, and other musicians. This is Jackson blurring the line between composer and songwriter; the textures presented are complex and heavily reliant on orchestral instruments, but the songs contained within the compositions are acerbic, sharp, and pointed allied with memorable melodies.

## 'Prelude' (2.59)
The CD booklet highlights a quotation from Robert Browning (1812-1889), the Victorian poet; 'The Devil, that old stager … who leads downwards, perhaps, but fiddles all the way'. It is the violin which is the focal point of this opening instrumental piece.

Beginning with a dramatic bass note from the piano, with sustained strings in the background, there is the occasional drum roll adding to the tension, and Nadja Salerno-Sonnerberg gives full voice to her solo, which is by turns anxious and then becomes beautifully playful.

At 1.27, there is a change of feel as organ, bass, and bongos provide a more relaxed tapestry for the intertwining string melody lines. The volume grows, as does the underlying tempo, becoming again unsettling whilst remaining flowing and melodic, building to a crescendo, and a reprise of the opening style. The piece ends with just the violin playing increasingly sporadic phrases, diminishing in volume and intensity, ending on a single sustained note which segues directly into…

## 'Fugue 1: More Is More' (Gluttony) (5.31)
A fugue is a musical composition where a short melody or phrase is introduced by one instrument or pitch, successively taken up by others, and developed by interweaving the parts.

Another dramatic opening, this one based around a fast and complex bass line where the string section joins in with an attacking, rhythmic counter melody. This busy mixture is joined by the piano and the music gathers pace, becoming ever more intense until, at 1.52, a new idea is introduced.

Stab chords are played in a staccato fashion under the strings and Jackson's (self harmonising) voice is heard leading into the first verse at 2.08. Immediately the lyrics hammer home their point; 'Let it rain, let it rain, let it rain, let it pour, we'll have one for the road, put the bolt on the door. Let it rain cats and dogs, let it rain rats and snakes, but just bring us more grog and another red steak'. A further verse doesn't lighten the tone; 'Let it rain, let it hail, let it rain frogs and toads, but just bring us some ale, we'll have ten for the road. Let it blow, let it roar, let it rain bats from Hell, wipe their arses and pluck 'em, we'll eat them as well.'

At 3.03, a new section appears. Here the percussion is largely absent, although the central melodic theme is retained as the lyrics shift towards Clyde, a man who ate himself to death despite the intervention of medical staff. Jackson's vocal melody keeps descending throughout the section where he is singing at the very bottom of his range by the end of the story. This temporary aural respite is soon over, with the initial heavy sounding music returning. The third verse has a great couplet summing up the song's subject matter; 'So who cares about Heaven, or burning beneath, when we're all busy digging our graves with our teeth'.

At 4.06, we have another morbid tale, this one concerning Matt who fell into a vat and died, although it took him a week as he 'kept getting out for a leak'. Again the vocal melody starts high and ends up very low indeed. The final verse (4.31), has another classic Jackson 'in character' rhyme; 'Give 'em two vegetarians and two of the poor, and two of the tossers who say less is more'. The music gathers pace to a frenetic level, gradually fading into a cacophony of sound effects.

## 'Angel' (Lust) (7.10)

'Angel' is also built around an ostinato played by the string section at a steady speed in 4/4, with solid support from percussion and piano. 'Angel' is a lady teasing men within her vision; 'Here's a young one, hey, Rufus, how's the rain on the rhubarb? All you need is a real girl guide, give it up and come inside. Slip the leash, shake it loose, bite the peach, suck the juice...'. Her lyrics are both spoken and sung by Suzanne Vega, the American singer-songwriter of 'Tom's Diner' and 'Left Of Centre' fame, with Jackson providing the harmonised vocals for the song's title.

There is a change in the texture at 2.00 where a quieter section (consisting primarily of strings is the background) with a section in Latin, the words based on 'Ave Gloriosa' by Philip the Chancellor and dating from the fourteenth century. This is sung by Dawn Upshaw, the American classical soprano.

The opening string riff, and Angel, then reappear; 'Hey chicken, is that your girl? Bet she lays like a lump ... You wanna walk in the dark with me, to a place where no-one sees? Kiss the glove, pretty please. You wanna pray? On your knees'. Another section of Latin occurs between 5.05 and 6.12, with the song concluding with Angel eyeing up another man as the music fades; 'Hey sailor, how's the steam in the stovepipe?'.

## 'Tuzla' (Avarice) (7.35)

'Tuzla' is a city in North-East Bosnia and Herzegovina. Initially, this appears to be an unusual subject matter for composition, but clues are given in the CD booklet where the two pages dedicated to the song's lyrics are printed over newspaper reports of the war (1992-1995), which followed the break up of Yugoslavia.

Floating in over a sustained synthesiser chord with a syncopated piano rhythm, some high-quality quasi-operatic warbling courtesy of Dawn Upshaw and some light percussion, the song soon settles into a repeating riff on the bass, with percussion and some deliberate interference providing another unsettled atmosphere.

Avarice (the more formal definition of greed) is exemplified in the song's opening couplet; 'Of all the treasure in our chest, we love the golden god of war the best'. This point is emphasised twice more in the composition; 'Of all the sterling men of steel, we crave the one who'll teach us not to feel' (3.16), and 'Through all the days and all the times, we count the coin and stash away the crimes' (5.57).

Jackson's contribution is both spoken and sung and is delivered with a degree of distortion to his voice which suggests it may have been recorded either via a telephone or a megaphone. He plays the part of the cynical observer, a reporter or a member of the armed forces, commenting on the desperate circumstances he sees; 'Look, look at that little clown. Here, look through the binoculars, someone burned his schoolhouse down and he's blinking in the sun. He's drying something in the sun. Ha! It's an old teabag! Now he rolls it up, look! He made a cigarette but he's not gonna smoke it yet. Maybe he's gonna sell it How much d'you think he'll get?'

'Normal'-sounding male and female voices continue the bleak diatribe; 'A slice of ham, a long goodbye, three days of peace. A bar of soap, a can of oil, ten years of debt. A pinch of salt, a week of news, four double A's. A plastic bag, a place to hide, one sucker bet'. This culminates in the powerful, harmonised section; 'I got what you want, I got what you need', all the while underscored by the continuous bass riff and percussion.

Jackson returns for more spoken analysis, this time focussing on a man selling beer to his mortal foe; 'It's not the time to kill, not that he forgets...as he takes a crumpled bill and thinks: this is better yet.' Another section of the male and female voices: 'A pot for the rain, a pair of shoes, two hand grenades. A spade for a grave, four lovely eggs, three cigarettes. A stick of gum, some wood for a fire, two table legs. A cup of rice, a pint of blood, one pound of flesh' leads to a reprise of the powerful harmonies; 'Line up to buy here, line up to die there'.

The final section of this unsettling song has Jackson turning his gaze towards a window. Appropriately the sound of militaristic drumming is added to the soundscape; 'Looks like your sister there in a Chetnik's bed. Look, there on the table, look's like she did it for a loaf of bread. Shit, she's got a knife! And he's snoring like a pig. Is he worth more alive or dead? How much for his boots? How much for his head?'

The hypnotic combination of the bass riff, relentless percussion, the changing vocal textures, the blend of spoken and sung words, and pizzicato strings creates a tense, foreboding feel throughout the track. The coda section has female vocals duetting in a celebratory fashion over the military drumming as the music fades into the distance.

## 'Passacaglia: A Bud And A Slice' (Sloth) (8.37)

A passacaglia is a composition of continuous variation in 3/4 time. Given the song's subject matter 'A Bud And A Slice' is taken at a suitably lugubrious tempo, with bass notes on the piano and a weighty drum and bass presence all contributing to the tired, lazy mood intended. A beautiful, sustained and harmonised bassoon part adds to the somnolent atmosphere. At 0.58, a new melody is added on the viola, being further harmonised by the cello. At 1.56, a new theme is introduced on electric piano, over which violin and viola add further layers. In the background, the slow, rollingly rhythmic backdrop continues.

At 2.52, the laconic, almost spoken vocals of Brad Roberts (singer with the Canadian band the Crash Test Dummies) are finally heard; 'Give me a Bud and a slice, and leave me alone. If I want your advice, I'll ask ya. They tell me that caviar's nice, but I wouldn't know. So what's it to you? Who needs your airs, and your microbrew?'

At 3.23 a new section, replete with pizzicato strings and swirling synthesisers, appears with an enchanting melody; 'Look at the sun, see how it hangs so still in the sky'. This brief respite is soon replaced with another, dour verse; 'Give me the new TV Guide and get off the phone, go on and take sides, it's not my problem. Waiting for worlds to collide in the comfort of home, they say Lucifer's free. What shall we do? Don't ask me'.

The pace quickens and the mood changes at 4.31 as Jackson appears in the guise of a new character, a man who took his daughter to see the 'new Tarantino'. At one horrific point in the film, the girl throws up only to be told by her father; 'It's just like the *Beano*, it's not real, and if it was... well, so what?' The section finally comes to a close with Jackson's imploring that we all 'lighten up!'

A final verse from Roberts with the pretty interlude ('Look at the sun...') brings the album's longest track to its close, with two sustained electric piano chords which are repeated are joined by a relaxed drum rhythm with added string harmonies on top as the music fades, as if falling into a torpor.

## 'Right' (Anger) 4.36

The album's shortest song is also the one which could be most closely aligned to the 'Angry Young Man' persona that the less intelligent corners of the music media tried to pigeonhole Jackson into early in his career.

It begins with a hesitant version of the melody from the song's third section played on an out-of-tune piano, which stops abruptly and someone, presumably Jackson, says 'Damn!' There then follows a fantastic sounding drum introduction played by Dan Hickey (in the left channel) and Kenny Aronoff (in the right). All tonal hell is unleashed thirty seconds in as a series of un-harmonic piano chords are slammed out on the relentless crotchet beat over which the following is shouted; 'Fuck this, bullshit, spit flat, beer back, rock star, dumb luck, sick joke, clap trap'. An excellent bass groove joins the mid-paced proceedings before another verbal, atonal onslaught; 'Damn thin, shoelace, yank spit, jerk snap, bomb kike, scam bank, tear down, dead flag'.

At 0.58 the song's next section is classic Jackson; 'I got a right to bite the hand that feeds the greed that pays the band, I got a right to fight the man that takes the cake that feeds the clan', the vocal melody soaring over the syncopated chord changes with the drummers having a great time by the sound of it. The vocal melody is echoed by the piano before the song drives into its third section.

At 1.34, there is the sound of a door slamming, the rest of the band sounds like they've been banished to an adjacent room, and a (this time) in tune piano takes up the introductory theme; 'I don't like the way you look at me, you don't like what I do in bed. Maybe I should get some deputies, and come and break your fucking head. Oh, no, no that won't do at all'.

A simple rising and falling D flat major scale is repeated and we are suddenly transported to Times Square where Jared Crawford (of percussion show *Stomp* fame) plays a vigorous solo on some plastic buckets amidst all the sounds of New York City. Against this backdrop a fourth section of vocals is heard; 'Ignorance is a kind of bliss, a smack in the mouth is a kind of kiss', as synthesisers provide a sustained accompaniment which builds back into the 'separate rooms' scenario; 'Methinks I doth protest too much, and no matter what the people say, I'm gonna have to get in touch with my inner adult someday...'.

At 3.32 there are two more verbal dissonant attacks, and the song enters its final furlong with another triumphant sounding verse; I got a right to light the flame that fries the guys that take the blame. I got a right to bite the hand that feeds the greed that pays the band'. The melody is again echoed by the piano and the bass groove takes us to an unexpected, dramatic ending on the fourth beat of the final bar.

## 'The Bridge' (Envy) (5.58)

After all the sound and fury of the preceding music, 'The Bridge' is the collection's ballad which sounds like it has been transported from any of Jackson's albums from *Night And Day* onwards to land here to provide six minutes of relative peace for the ears and mind. Synthesisers, piano, and bongos provide the background to Canadian singer-songwriter Jane Siberry's stunning performance of Jackson's poetic lyrics; 'Down there in the ashes there's gold and silver too. Dear sister, I try to share with you. 'Smug', you said, take your spoils away. And you broke the bridge on your side.'

Why a female voice was chosen over Jackson's distinctive style is unknown, but the effect is striking and atmospheric. The musical mood is of quiet contemplation; the strings rise and fall in dynamic support of the melodies, with the piano being the main instrumental voice. The song's mid-section (2.40-3.27) has an increase in the tension and volume, before the final verse; 'I fail with my anger and with my sympathy. I tremble, so little left for me. 'Harsh', you said, now you walk away. But I left the gold for you to find when you broke the bridge on your side'. The song's coda has Jackson's flowing, jazz-tinged piano lines rising in pitch as the percussion fades away, leaving just his isolated playing.

## 'Fugue 2: Song Of Daedalus' (Pride) (7.52)

The epic finale to *Heaven & Hell* is a composition of three distinct parts.

The first section ('Fugue 2') is a beautifully recorded string quartet with soaring violin and violas merging with a sonorous cello to produce an introduction like no other on the album. The dynamics rise and fall as the texture thickens, the melodies interweaving as the music grows and develops, dropping down again before another build into the second section, which begins at 1.58.

There is a sense of peace and calm to the backing for Jackson's vocals; 'Call me cool as January, I walk like the breeze and wear the world like filigree...'. The dynamics and tension grow before subsiding for the second set of verses; 'Call me irresponsible, your rules of the game are only clouds to float above...' The music recedes again for the next lyrics; 'Call me weird and laugh at me. I tell you it's true, I've found a cure for gravity...'

This time the music moves into a dramatic, sustained reprise of the vocal melody of 'More Is More'; 'See the wings made of feathers, of wax and of thread, see me soar high above all the quick and the dead'. This is a reference to the tale of Daedalus and Icarus in Greek mythology, where a father and his son used wings to escape from the island of Crete. Icarus fell from the sky when the wax that fastened the wings to his body was melted by the heat of the sun.

At this point (5.21), the strings become more agitated, increasing in pace and strength, then building into the powerful rising repeated three-chord conclusion; 'Call me now, call me stars and moon and plough, call me Lord, call me Sire, call me earth and wind and fire, call me Judge, call me Shah, call me King, call me Tsar, call me God'. Jackson's voice cracks on this final word as the music stops.

The third part of 'Song of Daedalus' is a brief reprise of the Prelude, a reprise of the neat trick that book-ended 'Night Music'. Over a sustained bass note and sustained violins, echoing piano chords appear in the left and then right stereo channels, with occasional distant phrases from the violin, before a long and peaceful fade.

# Symphony No.1

Personnel:
Joe Jackson: piano, keyboards, sampling, sequencing
Wessell Anderson: alto saxophone
Terence Blanchard: trumpet
Robin Eubanks: Trombone
Mary Rowell: violin, electric violin, viola
Steve Vai: electric guitar
Mat Fieldes: electric bass, acoustic bass guitar
Gary Burke: drums
Sue Hadjopoulos: percussion
Recorded and mixed at Avatar Studios, New York City
Dan Gellert: associate producer, recording engineer, mixing engineer
Sheldon Steiger: associate producer
Anthony Ruotolo: assistant recording engineer
Released: October 1999 on Sony Classical
Highest chart positions: did not chart

**On his website Jackson provides the following thoughts on *Symphony No. 1*:**

I'd always wanted to write a large-scale piece which had the structure of a symphony but wasn't written for an orchestra and didn't sound like 'classical' music. I'd been making sketches for years and I finally sat down and worked it all out. It wasn't as hard as you might think, it was easier for instance than *Heaven & Hell* because I didn't have to write lyrics or sing. I suppose it comes across as a kind of jazz-rock symphony and some people have compared it to Frank Zappa's instrumental stuff. I never expected it to have a big audience, but I think it was successful on three counts; one, I think it holds up and works as a composition; two, I got some fantastic musicians to play it and they were extremely supportive (Terence Blanchard, for instance, came up and hugged me at the end of the sessions, and Steve Vai became a friend) – and three, it won a Grammy, for Best Pop Instrumental Album, which is as good a category as any.

Normally the word 'symphony' is, as night follows day (again, sorry), followed by 'orchestra'. But as this is a Joe Jackson project, this convention is turned on its head in favour of an unusual line-up of instrumentalists. Jackson's last all-instrumental album, *Will Power*, was a collection of six individual pieces without thematic or melodic links. A symphony has a much more formalised, elaborate structure, usually in four movements, at least one of which is in sonata form; this being a musical structure with three main sections; an exposition, development, and recapitulation.

Bearing in mind that my cards are still in the same place as they were for *Will Power*, my comments on this album are written with my guitar teacher hat firmly in place. No further metaphors will be harmed in the writing of this review. I lay no claim to expertise on the construction, composition or performance of symphonic works. Jackson wrote the following performance notes for the CD, which do a far better job of explaining his themes and ideas than I can:

> It grew from a handful of ideas, for instance, that on the eve of the 21st century, a piece which was symphonic in structure surely didn't have to be written for a 19th-century orchestra to qualify as a symphony. I also had a handful of very simple musical themes in my head and wanted to see if they could be developed and transformed throughout four whole movements. Gradually I started to see the symphony as a person, like a character in a musical novel, travelling through four stages of life.

In reviewing the four movements of the symphony, Jackson's commentary precedes my own thoughts.

## 'First Movement' (17.20)

> The first movement emerges out of chaos with a saxophone solo which sounds improvised but actually contains the seeds of everything to come. The music then gradually coalesces into some sort of personality. The symphony is now a small child in C major with a tendency to slide into F sharp. The rest of the movement I see as a journey of discoveries; episodes both wondrous and frightening, puzzling then clear. Overall, though, a pattern is emerging. The climax of the movement is inspired by a memory; I am ten years old, running down the hill that overlooks my home town on a windy day, thrilled to be alive, feeling that ten is the perfect age to be, but at the same time that life stretches endlessly ahead of me. The movement subsides into a quiet coda, the end of childhood.

Given Jackson's contextualisation, this, the longest of the movements, makes sense. The music grows from nothing to involve numerous melodies played on combinations of saxophone, brass, violin, and guitar; sometimes intertwining, playing Jackson's syncopated, climbing phrases individually. There is a steady backing of percussion and drums almost throughout the movement, and plenty of moments where the instruments blend together in intensity and volume to produce some extremely effective climaxes.

Steve Vai's distinctive guitar tone becomes the dominant voice in the middle and latter thirds of the composition, with the most impressive section at around the twelve-minute mark. Here, to my mind, a child's sense of wonder, of endless possibilities and energy, captured with sustained distortion and some busy keyboard ostinatos. Some terrific crescendos at the fifteen-minute mark lead to a brief silence which is followed by a slower, more considered coda section; major chords underpin a minor key piano melody, and a low pitched tune on the viola signifies the end of the movement.

## 'Fast Movement' (7.03)

In the second (fast) movement the symphony has entered youth, so now it's both energetic and arrogant. This is a send-up of a symphonic scherzo. Scherzo literally means 'a joke', and there are lots of musical jokes and puns here. At this age, nothing is sacred, even (in the middle section) Beethoven.

The second movement is the most fun to listen to. Steve Vai, 'stunt' guitarist in Frank Zappa's bands during the 1980s and, at this point, probably the finest electric guitarist on the planet, has plenty to do in this entertaining composition. The fluid main melody is syncopated across differing time signatures, and the whole piece has a 'prog-rock' feel to it. Violin and piano join in the fun.

After the opening, there is a more reflective section (1.17) with the trumpet taking the lead, before the guitar barges back in and the drums really start rocking. The trumpet holds onto the melody in this second section behind a busy keyboard and percussion background. At 3.08 there is a momentary fanfare from the brass, joined by some typical 1970s sounding organ, before a complex build leads into a sustained guitar solo which bends into feedback before another break, and a repeat of the 'fanfare' motif. Percussion takes over, with high pitched keyboards developing the melodies, before a playful violin joins in. Trumpets and guitar bring the heavy drums in for a celebratory sounding conclusion with a tight repeated triplet ending.

## 'Slow Movement' (9.03)

The slow movement is a reflective period in mid-life. Sooner or later, we all have to deal with the 'D's; disillusion, depression, divorce, disease, death. Ideas from the previous two movements are turned over and re-examined from different angles. The trumpet solo is melancholy, but also contains hope, I think.

Despite its potentially despondent subject matter, the overall mood of the third movement is one of resigned tranquillity and sadness, rather than angst and anguish. After an opening involving a two-note piano interval, a slow and haunting melody appears on a slightly distorted electric guitar. Throughout the piece, Vai and Blanchard have substantial passages where their tone and technique is heard to its best advantage, whilst the piano and strings play a largely supporting role.

At times the harmonic textures and movement are reminiscent of some of the work of Broadway musical composer Stephen Sondheim (1930-2021).

Elsewhere there is a sense of other worldliness to the occasionally atonal, but rarely jarring melodies. The final section (from seven minutes onwards) features a supremely expressive trumpet solo which brings the music to an ending with a positive resolution.

## 'Last Movement' (10.16)

The last movement is a series of variations on a theme that has grown out of elements from all three previous movements. The variations travel alternatively from C to F sharp, and then from F sharp to C and form an arch (ABCDEFEDCBA) that ends in F sharp. This movement is a vision of what I would like to find in old age; clarity and balance, like a juggler keeping all the balls in the air, once again, simple joy in being alive'.

The alphabetical arch Jackson refers to is musical shorthand for identifying individual sections within a longer piece. (Fun fact: the title of Genesis's 1981 hit single 'ABACAB' was based entirely on this idea). The overarching mood of the movement is of balance and hope; the drums have a more permanent place in the soundscape (recalling their contribution to the first movement) and much of the music is in major keys.

The opening section recalls the texture and style of 'Only the Future' from *Night Music* and, whilst the final section of the symphony (subtitled 'Variations) features fragments and motifs of melodies that have appeared earlier, this is no straightforward reprise.

At 1.41, the electric violin is heard with a melodic development and at 2.27 there is an abrupt change of feel, as the brass instruments provide a more dissonant atmosphere than before. Another change of mood is signified by a sparse electric piano section which also features a melodic bass part. At 4.25 another outbreak of drums with some atonal brass brings to mind the texture and tension of parts of the musical *West Side Story*.

After a reprise of the electric piano section, the hopeful and light-hearted feel of the first movement is re-established with the horns harmonising with a syncopated piano and bass accompaniment. The electric violin also returns and at 7.50 the piano takes over with a celebratory sounding tune over a busier instrumental background. This moves into a 6/8 dance-style rhythm with a strong contribution from the electric violin. At 9.44 there is a brief pause followed by a single powerful piano chord which brings to mind the final seconds of 'A Day In The Life' by The Beatles (1967).

In *A Cure for Gravity: A Musical Pilgrimage*, Jackson wrote: 'So I'm still making music, no longer a pop star, if I ever really was, but just a composer, which is what I wanted to be in the first place'.

# Night And Day II

Personnel:

Joe Jackson: vocals, all keyboards, synth basses, sequencing and drum programming.

Sussan Deyhim: vocals ('Why')

Dale De Vere: vocals ('Glamour And Pain')

Marianne Faithfull: vocals ('Love Got Lost')

Alexandra Montano: 'Dying Diva' vocals ('Love Got Lost')

Mary Rowell: violin

Todd Reynolds: violin

Ralph Farris: viola

Dorothy Lawson: cello

Graham Maby: bass ('Glamour And Pain', 'Love Got Lost', 'Just Because…')

Sue Hadjopoulos: percussion ('Prelude', 'Hell Of A Town', 'Stranger Than You', 'Happyland')

Gary Burke: drums ('Love Got Lost')

Written, arranged, and produced by Joe Jackson

Don Gellert: Engineer and associate producer

Recorded at Avatar, New York City

Assisted by Charlie Post and Ross Peterson

Mastered by Ted Jensen at Sterling Sound

Released: October 2000 on Sony Classical

Highest chart position: did not chart

Prior to *Night And Day II* Jackson released his second live album in June 2000, *Summer In The City: Live In New York*. Drawing on material from three shows recorded at Joe's Pub in Manhattan in August 1999, it featured Jackson (piano, vocals), Graham Maby (bass, vocals), and Gary Burke (drums). The tracklisting was:

'Summer In The City', 'Obvious Song', 'Another World', 'Fools In Love'/'For Your Love', 'Mood Indigo', 'The In Crowd'/'Down To London', Medley 1: 'Eleanor Rigby'/'Be My Number Two'/'Home Town'/'It's Different For Girls', Medley 2: 'King Of the World'/You Can't Get What You Want (Till You Know What You Want')/'One More Time'.

If Jackson has a spirit animal, then it is surely a cat; independent, stubborn, prone to going off on adventures, always going to follow his own path, and eventually returning home. His retrospective view of *Night And Day II*, quoted on his website, was:

> I still don't know if the title was the right thing to do. The consensus seems to be, in retrospect, that it hurt rather than helped. But I went with it because there were so many connections to the earlier album. It's supposed to be

something like a day in the life of New York, seen through the eyes of several different characters. The tracks are continuous and all in the same tempo, though the actual grooves change around it. That was a technical trick which I felt worked very well, it seemed to give the whole thing a kind of relentless drive like the energy of a big city. And I loved working with Marianne Faithfull (on 'Love Got Lost'). Anyway, I reckon this is one of my best albums and certainly my most underrated.

*Night And Day* was a shimmering, near-perfect collection of songs that reflected Jackson's move to Manhattan. It sounded like the city, with plenty of Latin and pop accents as Jackson's trademark cynicism collided with a previously semi-submerged romantic streak. The enthusiasm and optimism of the 1982 release are in sharp contrast with the characters and situations portrayed here. Eighteen years on it's as if New York has worn the songwriter down, and this is evidenced by the cover. Eschewing the bright, stylish 'Art Deco' style of the first album, here we have a black and white, night-time shot taken from within a New York City cab, with the twin towers of the World Trade Centre in the foreground. A pensive looking Jackson is seen in the driver's rear-view mirror; the bright lights of the big city seemingly having little effect on him now.

Throughout most of the 'sequel' an electronic hi-hat rhythm pulses away relentlessly in the background, enabling each song to flow seamlessly into the next. This gives the impression that the album is a series of snapshots, each one focussing on different individual's stories and experiences of living in New York. Frustratingly this also keeps all ten tracks at the same middling tempo. As a result, *Night and Day II* doesn't capture the pace, excitement, or variety of the city like the first side of its predecessor did. Equally, the 'continuous tempo' idea, whilst clever and effective in moving the songs into each other, doesn't allow the album the luxury of the ballads, with the exception of 'Love Got Lost', to add some 'rise and fall' to the listener's experience.

## 'Prelude' (1.57)

Against a quiet background of some unspecific city sounds a hi-hat and claves fade in and out of the left and right channels, setting up a constant, agitated rhythm before being joined by a low, deep synthesiser note. Over this a graceful, legato cello melody soars over the soundscape, before subsiding, leaving the percussive rhythm segueing straight into...

## 'Hell Of a Town' (3.18)

A song containing the titular words, but entitled 'New York, New York' (no, not that one,) featured in the 1944 Broadway musical *On the Town* which gave us a tourist's wide-eyed enthusiasm for 'The Big Apple'. Jackson subverts this, putting the negative connotation on 'Hell'. His updated view of New York has 'smoke coming up through the holes in the ground', and 'plenty of devils for taking you down'.

Powered along by the percussion, a simple bass ostinato and short phrases from the violin and cello, Jackson's vocals build into the tense chorus; 'So get out of my goddam way, I'm walking here, I'm talking here'. We are a long way away from the exuberance and positivity of *Night and Day* despite some very similar instrumentation, especially in the non-vocal section, (1.30-2.09); this is a city by night where you'd better watch your step. As if to emphasise the point the final verse has the lines 'always room on the merry-go-round, so step up and be damned today'. The chorus is repeated, suddenly cutting off leaving just the percussion which leads straight into...

## 'Stranger Than You' (4.17)

'Stranger Than You' is the most 'Jackson-esque' song of this collection. The important elements are all here; the piano, a highly rhythmic backbone, the sardonic wit and eye for detail, and the sheer hummability of the melodies. Like 'Hell Of A Town' this song is written in the first person, and introduces us to a couple of the narrator's friends (The Chinese Elvis, and the Indian Jew), both of whom have 'colourful' lives. However, these are as nothing when compared to '...you, came along, thanks for opening my eyes, things you do, right or wrong, it should come as no surprise. When you live in a town, there's always somebody stranger than you'.

After the second chorus, Jackson turns listeners' expectations on their heads by admitting that 'I'm not complaining even though I'm not sure what you are, I've got the strangest feeling, good about this love bizarre'. By the end of the song, Jackson confesses to some confusion; 'Are you a boy, are you a girl? Are you an oyster, are you a pearl? Are you a fish, are you a fowl? Are you an angel, are you from hell?'

'Stranger Than You' has a strong, melodic chorus, and comes as a welcome 'blast from the past' for fans who had stuck with him through the musical twists and turns of *Night Music*, *Heaven & Hell,* and *Symphony No.1*. Here is a first-class example of 'Jackson the Songwriter', combining clever lyrics with compelling melodies and unusual instrumentation to produce a highly effective and individual 'pop' song.

## 'Why' (3.54)

The mood turns darker. Opening with some Eastern scale based melodies from the strings over the hi-hat, an anxious backdrop pulses behind Sussan Deyhim's vocals. The lyrics are short and sparse, and lay bare the concerns and confusions of immigrants of the city; 'Why smoke is coming out of ground? Tell me why? My English make an ugly sound, but I try. Why the Empire State Building green? Tell me why? Why house is smell of gasoline? Do I die?'

Interspersed with the words are some operatic style vocal swoops, which do nothing to dispel the inherent tension. There is a superb, low pitched cello solo (2.20-3.02) which blends into more quasi-operatic gymnastics for the long, drawn-out close to this intense, unsettling piece.

## 'Glamour And Pain' (5.59)

'Glamour And Pain' is the first song on the album to reference *Night and Day* directly. It's another song with piano, bass and percussion prominent along with drag queen Dale De Vere, who was apparently discovered by Jackson when his quest to get Jimmy Somerville (of The Communards fame) to sing the song, was unsuccessful. The vocalists' styles are very similar.

Jackson's words take us inside the world of a prostitute after a recent encounter with a client; 'Do you remember me, or just the shiny, shiny shoes I had you kiss for me? And my legs as smooth as chrome. Were you in ecstasy? As you were pumping out a flood of dollar bills for me?' In a live setting touring violinist Alison Cornell would take over the lead vocal duties and give a stunning performance of this powerful, moving composition.

At 2.32, the instantly recognisable two-note phrase from 'Steppin' Out' is quoted, and then repeated in a lower key before melding into an instrumental section with the melody in unison with the violins. After the third verse and chorus ('Hooray for Superwhore'), the 'Steppin' Out' motif reappears, complete with a key change and a reprise of the instrumental section. A further chorus has the music calming down a tinkling, simplistic, high pitched piano melody playing out over the fade, which crosses over into...

## 'Dear Mom' (4.12)

Built around an oscillating two-chord electric piano motif, and a counterpoint bass and keyboard melody with the ever-present hi-hat buzzing away in the ears, 'Dear Mom' is an affecting song concerning an absent sixteen-year-old girl. Narrated by the girl's brother each verse presents a different sighting, first somewhere 'downtown', then at the El Mocambo, where some guy said 'she put on quite a show'. Here the music grows in intensity into the chorus; 'What if she won't come home, you know she don't want your money, what if she won't come home?'.

The third verse finds the girl on the subway ('she got a new tattoo') where brother and sister converse; 'She swears she's gonna call me later, I'd say there's nothing we can do'. Another chorus is, again, followed by a brief instrumental before the final, depressing verse; 'Dear Mom, I heard from my little sister. Guess what? She's doing really well. She told me to give you a message for her; 'Dear Mom, why don't you go to hell?''

The final choruses add to the despair the parent must be feeling, as the brother too decides to stay in New York and not return home. The instrumental section is extended with the omnipresent hi-hat moving the music straight into the next song...

## 'Love Got Lost' (6.59)

There is an introduction consisting of repeated three bars of 4/4 time with a prominent keyboard melody and then, for once, the hi-hat rhythm disappears and the time signature moves into a swaying 6/8. But underneath this apparent change, the underlying tempo is unaltered, maintaining the sense of over-familiarity between all the songs.

This criticism aside 'Love Got Lost' is a beautiful song, with Marianne Faithfull giving a full-blooded, emotive performance of Jackson's lyrical depiction of a lonely middle-aged woman. The second verse is the best example; 'Saturday night, went to see *La Boheme*, used the spare ticket just for my coat, I guess I should swallow my pride, but I'll be damned if I'd hawk it outside in the pouring rain'. The character's loneliness is further emphasised with 'I'd like a new body and face, but I'd settle for a friend with a space on their calendar'.

The song's chorus is one of Jackson's best, recalling a time earlier in the lady's life; 'Long ago and far away, I was safe and sound, but love got lost along the way'. The sustained strings and gentle bassline add much to her sense of loss and the constant passage of time. Faithfull's interpretation of Jackson's melody has just the right amount of regret and longing to it, without coming across as bitter. The introduction is briefly reprised before the flowing 6/8 feel is restored.

A new section (4.01-4.45) finds the lady back in her office, and a man is interested in her. She can't decide how to react; 'Here comes Mr Worldly and Wise, if he touches me again, I'll scream. I can't stand his sensitive eyes, like I'm some dying diva to him, touch me, don't touch me...' This leads into a powerful 'instrumental' section in 9/8 time where the sound of a 'dying diva' is provided by Alexandra Montano (4.46-5.20), then a more reflective piano solo appears, playing the verse melody. The music subsides again for a final chorus before the 4/4 structure is reinstated with repeats of the introductory theme, which fades away, leaving just the hi-hat and some quiet indistinct whispering as the link into...

## 'Just Because...' (4.45)

The violins, viola and cello reappear with sparse, staccato phrases recalling aspects of *Heaven & Hell*, their lines gradually coalescing, becoming a growing, intense Baroque-style fugue which finally settles something akin to a riff by 1.20. This ostinato effectively captures the hustle and bustle of a busy city with no one having time for anyone else and everybody in everyone else's way.

Drums join the rhythm and Jackson's vocals are treated with a very short, slapback delay; 'Can't drink the water, can't breathe the air, can't hide down in the sewer 'cause there's crocodiles down there'. The chorus (2.05-2.42) distorts Jackson's voice (two bars of 6/4 time, followed by two bars of 4/4, which is repeated) and the well-known maxim; 'Just because you're paranoid, don't mean they're not out to get you.'

This refrain fades away against the agitated sounding backing and a second verse appears; 'Don't look at me on the subway and I won't look at you. Don't touch me with your greasy gloves and syphilitic flu...'. Another chorus (with Jackson's refrain again disappearing) leaves Maby's bass and distorted synthesisers backed by busy drums playing an instrumental coda, the instruments receding as the hi-hat continues yet again...

## 'Happyland' (5.12)

This song is inspired by the true story of a nightclub fire in the Bronx in 1990, although Jackson is at pains in the CD sleeve notes to emphasise that 'No connection is implied, nor disrespect intended to any persons living or dead'.

A simple, high pitched piano melody played in octaves rides over a wash of synthesiser, hi-hat, and claves. Jackson's lyrics describe a girl who was at a nightclub 'a year ago today'. Her partner, 'calm and handsome', 'wore a satin shirt and said a prayer to Yemaya', the water goddess in Afro-Caribbean religion. With his usual eye for detail Jackson captures the scene; 'The girls were in tight dresses, just like sweets in cellophane', whilst one has 'in her hand a single rose, in her mouth a razor blade'. The chorus rises up with an excellent melody and chord progression ('She says 'It was our night, watch us seize the day and dance it all away, bailamos, esta noche baliamos in Happyland') before relaxing back into the second verse.

Except the second verse is far from relaxed; a fire takes hold in the club, 'and then they heard the screams and saw the smoke come down'. Jackson isn't above using the blackest of humour at this point; 'And then it really turned into the hottest club in town'. The girl escapes but her partner does not, she sees the fire trucks and the media reporting the disaster. Realising that he is still inside the girl wants to go back in and rescue him; 'And people say she's loca to go back into that place'. A second chorus ('watch me seize the day' this time) is repeated, and the music calms again with Jackson's repeated occasional 'Happyland's, as the percussion begins to fade and the final song begins...

## 'Stay' (5.47)

More background city noise, some gentle piano and the hi-hat wandering in and out of the mix amongst cymbal splashes, an electric piano requoting 'Steppin' Out', again in two different keys and a slow descending arpeggio lead into Jackson's reverb-drenched vocals, the ambience recalling 'Drowning' from *Laughter & Lust*.

Again, Jackson's lyrics are poignant and detailed; 'Here darkness never quite descends. Only the toughest stars hang with neon friends over neon candy stores 'till the bitter end'. The chords keep progressing downwards under the lyrics, the atmosphere brooding and apprehensive. In the second verse Jackson believes one day he will go mad 'raising a champagne glass down some dark alleyway, down some mean magnetic streets...'. It is this madness which focuses the chorus; 'You could live anywhere you want to, give me one reason to stay'. Unusually the chorus moves into waltz time (3/4), away from the relentless 4/4 of the verses.

A third verse, replete with more 'Steppin' Out' piano and percussion in and out of the background, paints a further depressing view; 'Here, monsters walk the earth again, mermaids in black and gold, perfume and cocaine, rising from a teeming sea, asking me again...'. At the end of the chorus, Jackson decides, in a long slow vocal phrase 'I think I'll stay'. Elements of the backing texture become sparser in the mix, all apart from the hi-hat, which, cockroach-like, survives when all the other instruments have faded into the darkness of this atmospheric song.

# Volume 4

Personnel:
Joe Jackson: vocals, piano, organ, electric piano, melodica
Gary Sanford: guitar, vocals
Graham Maby: bass, vocals
Dave Houghton: drums, vocals
Written and produced by Joe Jackson
Recorded by Julie Gardner at Ridge Farm, Surrey, England
Assisted by Helen Atkinson
Mixed by Sean Slade and Paul Kolderie at The Magic Shop, New York City
Assisted by Juan Garcia
Mastered by Ted Jensen at Sterling Sound, New York City
Released: March 2003 on Rykodisk
Highest chart position UK: 116, USA: 8

Prior to the arrival of the surprise 'Joe Jackson Band Reformation' album, in 2002 Jackson released his third live album, *Two* Rainy *Nights*, recorded in Seattle, Washington, and Portland, Oregon in April 2001. Playing a mixture of (very) new and some career-spanning older tracks the musicians were Jackson (piano, keyboards, vocals,) Graham Maby (bass, vocals), Sue Hadjopolous (percussion), Allison Cornell (violin, vocals, keyboards), Roberto Rodriguez (drums), Andy Ezrin (keyboards), and Catherine Bent (cello). The songs are:

'Prelude'/'Hell Of A Town', 'You Can't Get What You Want ('Till You Know What You Want'), 'Happyland', 'Stranger Than You', 'Another World', 'Is She Really Going Out With Him?', 'Home Town', 'Stranger Than Fiction', 'Glamour And Pain', 'Target', 'Just Because...', 'Got The Time', 'A Slow Song'.

Writing on his website regarding the reunion album Jackson said:

> I think I was a bit burned-out on big, complex projects at this point, and ready to strip things down. I wanted this to be the great fourth album my original band would have made if we'd stayed together a couple more years. I think it turned out to be even better than that, because of all the experience I'd gained as a writer and we'd all gained as players. For me this is far and away the best Joe Jackson Band album . . . though of course, you can't compete with nostalgia, no matter what you do.

Initial copies of *Volume 4* included a 'Special Bonus CD', which was a live recording from 2002, at The Marquee in London, and the Wedgewood Rooms in Portsmouth. The tracklisting was:

'One More Time', 'Is She Really Going Out With Him?', 'On Your Radio', 'Got The Time', 'It's Different For Girls', 'I'm The Man'.

With this album, Jackson, having got in through the cat flap, now headed for a familiar bed...

*Volume 4* is a cracking album and a welcome return to the style of songwriting with which Jackson first established himself; waspish, clever lyrics, great grooves, memorable choruses, and eleven really good, new songs. It's not an exercise in nostalgia. Jackson's lyrics are coloured by a further twenty years' experience, but he has not mellowed; if anything, his songs are all the better for the time that has passed since *Beat Crazy*. The recorded sound is excellent, direct, powerful and clear, and there is a sense of genuine pleasure with the four musicians reuniting and carrying on where they left off, rather than just replaying past glories.

## 'Take It Like a Man' (3.24)

Beginning with a thunderous blast of energetic drums and bass, Sanford's overdriven guitar, and Jackson's falsetto, the music is suddenly broken up by an isolated, repeated piano riff which is joined by guitar, and then the vocals break loose over the full band rhythm.

A song about the switch in the male/female power dynamic ('Don't let her down, just 'cause you could before, she stole the crown, you don't rule anymore') has Jackson emphatically taking the woman's side; 'You feel her touch, fingers like icicles, she needs you so much, like fish need bicycles', with the chorus refrain underlining this; 'Oh no, take it like she did before. Oh no, take it like a man'.

Brisk, edgy, and bristling with energy 'Take It Like A Man' is an excellent opener, a statement of intent for the rest of the album. The piano, guitar, bass, and drums are perfectly mixed, harmony vocals are clear, and the song powers itself to a sustained chord ending.

## 'Still Alive' (3.43)

'Still Alive' is a slower song which raises the bar still further. It has more than a flavour of 'Ticket To Ride' by The Beatles (from their 1965 album *Help!*) in its syncopated drum rhythms, chiming guitar arpeggios, tempo, and vocal harmonies. These comments are not to criticise or imply plagiarism, merely to identify the elements that really work in making this track such a compelling and commercial composition.

Sanford's guitar sounds superb, and Jackson gives an 'emerging from the wreckage' analysis of a now-dead relationship. Whilst mourning the loss, he is proud of his ability to survive the emotional carnage; 'You turned me upside down and turned my insides out but that's alright'. This opinion is reinforced with the excellent chorus; 'But something keeps on beating in there, I guess my heart survived. I know I said I couldn't live without you, but I'm still alive'.

A second verse in a similar vein follows and, as with a lot of Jackson's songs, the respective sexes are not specified in the lyrics. 'Still Alive' can be appreciated from both a male or female standpoint or, indeed, any point in between.

The bridge shifts key and briefly takes us back to the start of the relationship; 'In the beginning, we were there till the end of time. It isn't sinning to prepare for the kind of murder that's not a crime'. A climbing melody on the piano and melodica provides a short instrumental interlude, before the third verse and chorus. The lush harmonies of the repeated refrain 'Still Alive' blend with a return of the rising instrumental melody as the song fades.

## 'Awkward Age' (3.23)

In an interview with *ICE* in January 2003 Jackson said:

> I saw a 15-year-old girl in a railway station and tried to imagine if I was talking to her what I would say. The song starts off saying you're having all kinds of problems cause you're at an awkward age. But then it says well wait, I still have a lot of those problems, maybe we're all living at an awkward age. The bridge talks about how we're all under so much pressure from the media and marketing to be cool and thin and flawless. Though I wouldn't want to be 15 again, we're all having the same struggles.

The tempo picks up for this retrospective tale of how teenage experiences are carried throughout adulthood. The song opens with the terrific couplet; 'I should have known you were only just fifteen, you had a scowl like a Klingon beauty queen'. This is someone who is 'uncomfortable in their messed-up skin', a person who can't get into the 'cool parties'; Jackson relates to being 'left high and dry, don't cry, you're just at an awkward age.'

The chorus is another corker with a driving rhythm, a descending chord progression, falsetto vocals, and excellent harmony singing in the background. Fast forward to the present and the first person for the second set of verses ('I really thought by now a few things might just clarify' and 'I get into the parties but I hate them 'cause I'm shy') with Jackson concluding 'I'm still at an awkward age'.

The bridge section recalls elements of 'It's All Too Much' (from *Laugher & Lust)* with 'We're supposed to be happy, supposed to be tough, supposed to be flawless and buy the right stuff. They want us all swimming, don't care if we drown, so don't let them take you down'. Sanford's short guitar solo reprises the verse melody which leads into a final chorus with repeated 'Awkward Age's bringing the song to an end.

## 'Chrome' (4.22)

'Chrome' is the album's first ballad, not in terms of tempo but in the dynamics of the instruments, rim-shot drum rhythm, and the relaxed vocal delivery. Lyrically Jackson has in his sights a person who, when younger, always was 'the special one, the breath of air, the heap of fun. You always had a kind of light that might dismay, or might delight'. Someone who Jackson, singing in the first person, hoped would 'be mine', but doubted the reality of this ever happening.

Come the chorus and we discover that the person is now an international star and not only shines but is also hard and cold like chrome'. Each time the word 'chrome' is heard an extra level of reverb appears, extending the 'tail' of the sound. It's a clever production touch and stands out in the album where the intention has been to capture the band as clearly, crisply, and naturally as possible.

The second verse has Jackson wryly commenting; 'I know your age but I won't tell' after complimenting the person on their appearance. Another chorus is followed by an instrumental section (2.45-3.30) which initially throws the spotlight on Maby's melodic bass playing before veering off into jazzier territory for its second half. A repeat of the chorus and a reprise of the introduction lead to a slowing down of the tempo and a calm conclusion.

## 'Love At First Light' (4.08)

This is a classic example of Jackson's ability to write involving slower songs. Quieter still than 'Chrome', and the first song of the collection to move away from the default 4/4 time signature of much guitar-based rock music, 'Love At First Light' swings along in 3/4 with piano, brushes, restrained bass and gentle guitar arpeggios in the background.

Another first-person song finds Jackson watching, at 'the crack of noon', someone sleeping after a night of passion. Worried that he can't remember their name he is relieved 'when you awake and you flash me a smile like a diamond'. The vocal melody and Jackson's tone here are perfect. At this moment, he almost believes in 'love at first light'.

The second verse recalls the night before, using vampires as a metaphor. This is followed by a piano-based instrumental (2.17-2.35), which moves away from the song key of A major, passing through C major and Eb major, before returning to A major for the final verse.

Here we are back in the 'present' whilst maintaining the vampire references; 'Let's open the curtains and let out the dark, and if the sun doesn't melt us and there's still a spark, and we do something human-like walk in the park, the spark could ignite', with Jackson hoping that he's 'crazy enough to believe in 'love at first light''. The song fades with some melodic piano phrases over the still restrained backing.

## 'Fairy Dust' (3.48)

An angry wah-wah guitar riff accompanied by agitated drums and a busy bass line break the mood. This fast rocker, with tinges of jazz around the sides, is in 5/4 time throughout.

Lyrically this is Jackson taking on the unpleasant characteristics of a homophobe; 'Here, see the little queer, there's a volunteer, don't you think he should get a haircut now. Like in the marines, all the magazines got a way for everyone to shape up'. This is underlined in the words of the second chorus; 'Calling for the man of steel to blow you faggots into fairy dust'.

116

At 1.35, a jazz-rock style instrumental appears, with a frantic piano solo over the energetic band backing. This calms down at 2.14 with a quieter yet still tense piano riff to which is added vigorous percussion, more wah-wah guitar, and a brooding bass line. Verse three breaks in at 2.52 with Jackson in defiant mood; 'We're happy to be gay, showing you the way, gotta get your head, your heart, your torso hard'. After the third chorus, the song concludes with a highly discordant piano chord.

## 'Little Bit Stupid' (3.28)
In the same *ICE* interview, Jackson said:

> It's a very deliberate tribute to glam-rock from the '70s. The first bands Graham and I were in, we were playing all that stuff: early Bowie, Marc Bolan, Gary Glitter. I always liked glam, even though it was trash.

There is more than a hint of 'Glam Rock' about 'Little Bit Stupid', led by its boisterous drum rhythm, overdriven guitar, distorted bass, and catchy melodies, especially in the chorus; 'I have to say that we were suited, but you know what they say about Cupid, 'little bit stupid'. And like the early '70s musical movement it imitates, 'Little Bit Stupid' is a slice of lightweight, frothy fun with some great verse lines including 'Maybe too much lipstick made your mouth go dumb', and 'Or maybe too much mascara made my eyes go blind'.

Eschewing the expected guitar solo, Jackson throws in a short bluesy piano solo before repeated choruses. There is a brief homage to 'Blockbuster' by Sweet (1973) at 3.04, where Jackson intones 'We just didn't know what to do', as the song fades away.

## 'Blue Flame' (5.23)
Things turn more serious with the album's last ballad. A laid back pace, sparse guitar and restrained piano and bass provide a tranquil backing to Jackson's poetic lyrics; 'I've got some walls around me too, but they're not much compared to your house. Fifty feet high with barbed wire, guards on the top, aiming rifles at your lovers one by one, and friends too.'

Jackson wants to re-establish a relationship with the person (he recalls an 'evening when you smiled at something'), but there are limits; 'I've come with hands above my head. But I'm damned if I'll try to break your door down'. The section leading into the chorus is even better, as the music grows in intensity; 'Sadness spreads like a black stain. But I know by now, that's not all there is', as in the chorus Jackson explains 'there's a blue flame inside of you, so beautiful and rare. Love's not something we decide to do. You'd be so hard to love if love was not just there'.

Jackson's frustration with the object of his affection is detailed further in the third verse; 'I wonder what world you call home, and I wish I could learn their language just enough to make you laugh, just one time'. For the fourth verse, the two have met, but doubts remain; 'Yes, it was nice to see you too, although I'm never sure you mean it. I pick up the tab, and you won't thank me, not that I mind. But in my dreams it's all so different, we even kiss...'.

The music rises and falls for the chorus, but never more than that and fortunately never turning into that most predictable of creatures, the 'power ballad'. In less skilled hands walls of sound would reinforce the narrator's issues, but here the band remain restrained, letting the song work through subtlety rather than hammering the message home with distortion and stadium shaking drums.

'Blue Flame' is your quintessential Jackson ballad; melodic and yet hard-edged, lyrical and pointed, and performed with a style and control which set a standard few can match.

## 'Dirty Martini' (4.51)

A great, sleazy guitar riff and a relentless rhythmic groove provide the backbone for this mood changing song which moves out of its 4/4 time for an instrumental section between the verse and chorus. This consists of a bar of 4/4 followed by a bar of 5/4 which is played three times, over which a distorted guitar and melodica melody is heard.

The chorus ('Too many olives and too much gin, steppin' out in the City of Sin. Too much dirty rice and too many beans, gettin' down and dirty in New Orleans') is another cracker, and before the second verse, Jackson breaks into an unexpected impersonation of a werewolf. The backing vocals in the verse ('Dirt, dirt, dirty martini') and chorus are excellent, and Jackson's honky-tonk-esque piano solo in the instrumental section recreates the late night/early morning club atmosphere well.

The final chorus finishes at 3.35 but the coda runs for a nearly a further minute and a half and, like the drunk at the bar who refuses to go home, duly outstays its welcome.

## 'Thugs'R'Us' (3.23)

Evoking the 'Two Tone' movement, which swept through British pop music in the late Seventies, 'Thugs'R'Us' is an up-tempo number. Sharp staccato guitar chords and a bubbling bass line provide an appropriate accompaniment to the lyrics which sound both out of time and place. If this song, or something similar, had featured on *Beat Crazy* it would have fitted right in; here it's a wiser, older Jackson who sounds embarrassing, criticising today's youth, who 'wear hoods and baggy trousers on the bus.'

It's not a bad song by any means; it's just the underachiever in an otherwise superior class of songs. Lyrics like 'We got wide-arsed hippie mums. We look smart, but we wanna be dumb', and 'We got tight-arsed drippy Dads. We look good but we wanna be bad' aren't exactly Jackson's finest work. The best couplet in the track comes towards its close after the haunting melodica solo; 'We got beer but we want some crack. We look white, but we wanna be black'.

## 'Bright Grey' (4.17)

If this song has an antecedent then it is 'Got The Time', the similar final track on *Look Sharp!*. 'Bright Grey' is the fastest song of the collection and is reliant on triple rhymes in its depiction of a long term relationship going south; 'She says that he's pouring fuel on the fire. He turns around and calls her a liar. She says, 'I'm trying to get to a higher... place'. The second verse is less successful; 'He says that she's jealous just like a female. She says I caught you I went through your email. He says it's getting so hard just to be male...'. Here, the wordplay on 'male' and 'mail' doesn't work well and sounds forced.

The sound is delightfully thrashy, but luckily, strong melodies and clever chord progressions are never far away. This is particularly evident in the high energy chorus; 'Hey, why doesn't someone say, this dull black and white should fall away, Please, tell me it's not just me, can't wait until we're all bright grey'.

In the third verse, things have not improved for the couple; 'She packs her bags and goes home to mother. He says to go on cause he's sick of being smothered. She says I'm saving revenge for another ... day'. Another chorus is over by 2.35, and the song could have ended there. Instead, a manic, atonal guitar chord sequence forms an instrumental section (2.36 - 3.06) and leads to two reprises of the chorus. The coda is a repeat of the introduction, with the final four bars featuring a rising bass line to a final rasping chord.

# Rain

Personnel:
Joe Jackson: vocals, piano
Graham Maby: bass, vocals
Dave Houghton: drums, vocals
Written and produced by Joe Jackson
Recorded by Julie Gardner at Planet Roc, East Berlin
Assisted by Yensin Jahn
Mixed by Sean Slade and Paul Kolderie at The Magic Shop, New York City
Assisted by Ted Young
Mastered by Bob Ludwig at Gateway, Portland, Maine
Released: January 2008 on Rykodisk
Highest chart position UK: 154, USA: 133

Following the release of *Volume 4* the Joe Jackson Band toured across Great Britain, North America, Europe, and Australia for a year from September 2002. From this emerged a live album *Afterlife* recorded over four nights in August 2003 at three venues in California. The track listing was:

'Steppin' Out', 'One More Time', 'Take It like A Man', 'Awkward Age', 'Look Sharp!', 'Down To London', 'Beat Crazy', 'Fools In Love' (incorporating 'For Your Love'), 'Love At First Light', 'Fairy Dust', 'Sunday Papers', 'Don't Wanna Be Like That', 'Got The Time'.

Commenting on *Rain* on his website Jackson said:

Like *Volume 4* I think this was partly a reaction against the very ambitious projects I'd done a few years before, but even more stripped-down. I wanted to create something powerful with what I thought would be the absolute bare minimum of forces that I could do it with: just piano, bass, drums, and voices. It's interesting what happens when you take out the guitar, it seems to get bigger rather than smaller, there's a lot more space and the piano sounds huge. I think the album has a kind of timeless quality which I'm very pleased with.

The return of Jackson to his 'roots' (as far as his fans were concerned) was well received. Leaving behind entirely his alter ego of the 'The Serious Composer', *Volume 4* had been full of pithy, intelligent pop-rock which, whether he liked it or not, seemed, from both the fans and critics perspectives, to be his forte. Jackson never intended *Volume 4/Afterlife* to be anything other than a 'one-off' and, to an extent, this was true. With 'Rain' Jackson dispensed with the services of Gary Sanford and his guitar.

Talking about the album's title Jackson said, in an interview with *Clash Music. com* in January 2008, Jackson said:

I wanted something elemental because that's the kind of album I wanted to make. There is no padding on it at all; the album is stripped to the bare essentials, so I hope it has a timeless quality. The title seems to fit. It seemed like rain was a constant companion. It always seemed to be raining when I was working on these songs, and it rained every day while we were recording them. But I like the rain, and I don't understand why for many people it has this automatic association with doom and gloom. What would we do without rain?

*Rain* is smoother, more sonically mature, and lacking in some of the frantic moments which had appeared on the two 'Band' albums. It's sophisticated, yet still edgy, and oozes style and confidence. At times *Rain* has the feel of *Body and Soul* with its degree of polish and imagination, and reducing the band to a trio certainly emphasises the importance and quality of Jackson's piano playing. Lyrically he remains sharp, whether it's the observation of his own retreat from stardom ('Invisible Man'), contemplating photogenic non-conformists ('Good Bad Boy'), or commenting on hedonism ('King Pleasure Time'). But there is room too for romance with 'Wasted Time', 'Rush Across the Road', and 'Too Tough' all being particularly effective in combining a mixture of heartfelt honesty with the maturity of years.

The absence of the electric guitar inevitably means that the almost 'built-in' nostalgia element accompanying *Volume 4* is gone. Here Jackson shows in a stripped-down trio format that, yet again, his lasting strengths are as a songwriter and bandleader. After 30 years in the profession, he hasn't run out of ideas or invention.

Early pressings of the CD included a bonus DVD with performances of 'Invisible Man', 'Wasted Time', and 'Good Bad Boy' recorded at the Islington Academy, London in front of an appreciative audience. The DVD also featured interviews with Jackson, Maby and Houghton, a very short documentary on the making of *Rain*, and Jackson giving a good impression of a tour guide in Berlin, a city he had called home since January 2007.

## 'Invisible Man' (5.03)
In an interview with *Rock'n'Reel* in March 2008 Jackson said:

I think losing anonymity is a dangerous thing for an artist. I read an interview, years ago, with Joni Mitchell where she said when she became successful she changed from being an observer to being observed, and that this was very unhealthy for her creative process. I kind of agree with that. 'Invisible Man' from the new album is about how it's better to be more anonymous, which sort of goes against the grain of this celebrity-obsessed culture we have now.

The 'new sound' is laid out right from the off; Jackson's piano sounds full, rounded, and magnificent. Maby's bass provides the reassuringly smooth bottom end, whilst Houghton's drums are crystal clear, with plenty of air around their sound.

The introduction is based on three sets of four-bar phrases. Despite the time signature (4/4), the syncopation of the chords creates an unsettled, almost jazzy opening which doesn't settle until the pattern has been played eight times, and the music moves into a new theme:

Set One: One beat rest. A dotted crotchet C minor chord is followed by a dotted crotchet D minor chord.
Set Two: An Eb major chord is played on the first beat and sustains for five crotchet beats.
Set Three: An F major chord is played on the second beat, and sustains for four crotchet beats, effectively invading the first beat rest of Set One.

Jackson's heavily reverberated vocals begin on the third repeat of the series; 'Hey, can you hear me now, as I fade away and lose my ground? Maybe you'd like to know what I'd have to say, if I was still around?'

A very pretty quaver-based piano melody, akin to a child's music box, introduces a new, more relaxed section with Jackson's voice moving into falsetto; 'Now I'm made of smoke, you see through me, it's the strangest joke'. This then powers into the louder, driving chorus, where the backing vocals of Maby and Houghton are excellent. This section is also built around three sets of four-bar phrases which are played three times.

A single bar of 4/4 leads into a reprise of the introduction and the second verse with Jackson reflecting on the nature of fame and his place in it; 'Why did the lights go down, or onto someone new? Well, let them learn. I used to own this town, now I'm watching you, now it's my turn'.

The 'music box' section ('Now, I'm made of mist, will you know when you've been kissed?') follows. An instrumental section which is the introduction again has some impressive drum fills, and this moves quickly into the pre-chorus section; 'Now, I'm almost free, disappearing, don't cry for me'. Repeated choruses with the vocals appropriately fading away as the music continues at the same volume lead back to a brief recap of the introduction as a coda.

'Invisible Man', when it gets going (especially in the chorus) is quite the rocker, and the thought occurs; WWSP? What Would Sanford Play? It would be intriguing to hear the more powerful songs in this collection benefiting from some overdriven guitar. Or perhaps that's just me.

## 'Too Tough' (4.37)

A slower number with a loping, bluesy feel, the central two-bar piano riff is mirrored by a two-bar vocal line imitating the traditional 'call & response' structure of blues music. This theme changes for the pre-chorus, where another attractive piano arpeggio structure appears, with Maby's bass adding much to the mood. The chorus is another great one, with the relentless, repeated high crotchet 'D's acting as an effective drone against Jackson's full-throated 'rise and fall' melody.

The second verse has an excellent couplet; 'You've really gotten underneath my skin. Must have been easy it was always thin'. In the pre-chorus the lines 'But even when you're high, I can feel your pain, that's what I call being alive' also hit home. A piano led instrumental (2.24-2.42) introduces a bridge section, a return to the introduction, and the third verse. The pre-chorus has the memorable words; 'And it took a lot of time to grow your shell, maybe enough's enough. And I could tell you why you should go to hell, but I don't want to be that tough'. A reprise of the high class chorus and the introduction brings the song to a close.

## 'Citizen Sane' (4.21)

An up-tempo, stomp-a-long rhythm with a punky piano feel (hmm, this could be a new genre I've invented) means parts of 'Citizen Sane' are reminiscent of the more melodic moments of XTC. A coincidence to be sure, but Jackson is certainly a fan as was witnessed by his contribution to the album *A Testimonial Dinner – The Songs of XTC* issued in 1995. Jackson covered 'Statue of Liberty', first issued as a single by the band in 1978.

The music calms slightly for the pre-chorus ('He can put you on, or get you off, of the drug du jour...') before a rising chord progression brings us to the chorus itself which grooves along with a splendid, chugging bass line. A second verse, pre-chorus and chorus, is followed, predictably, by the bridge section (1.47-2.47), which features some excellent falsetto vocal lines. This builds to a terrific crescendo in its last few seconds, followed by a brief pause.

It's the opening section of the third verse which brings XTC to mind (2.56-3.16). A third verse/pre-chorus/chorus pattern leads into a brief coda which develops the earlier rising chord progression still further as the music fades away.

## 'Wasted Time' (5.11)

'Wasted Time' is another effortlessly classy Jackson ballad. The mood is set straight away with the slow melodic piano chords, and bittersweet lyrics; 'Maybe it would be better if we never said goodbye, maybe I'd grow much older with you in my life'. Rim-shot led drums add to the melancholy mood, and the second half of the verse sees Maby adding additional weight in the lower register.

Jackson's reflective singing and addictive melody capture the doubt and regret of his words perfectly. The music builds in intensity for the first half of the chorus (which, again, features a falsetto vocal), with some gorgeous backing harmonies appearing in the more introspective second half. The second verse is even better; 'After the party's over, after the dream has died, some people keep returning to the scene of the crime. Try to rewrite the story, tell you "you never tried". Tell you "you should be sorry" for wasting their time'.

The bridge section (3.19-4.08) modulates from A flat into a new key of B minor, with Jackson musing on making the best of the time available. The chord progression and vocal melody has vague echoes of *Pretzel Logic*-era Steely Dan to it, building to an effective crescendo. A strong repeat of the introduction leads into a final chorus, coming to a rest on a non-tonic chord of B major seventh.

## 'The Uptown Train' (5.46)

Here is a track which is either an instrumental with a relatively short lyrical section appearing in the middle or a song with a very long introduction and play-out, take your pick. Jackson admits in the accompanying DVD interview to taking inspiration for 'The Uptown Train' from the Ramsey Lewis Trio's 1965 version of 'The In-Crowd' (he refers to it as a 'blatant rip off'), and the similarities (tempo, instrumentation, and groove) are here for all to hear.

Whereas the former is entirely instrumental Jackson's composition grooves along effortlessly for nearly a minute and a half before the vocals appear, his barbed words aimed at an unnamed individual. Again, Jackson sings in falsetto, dropping into his usual register for the chorus; 'You've changed, they say. You can know when to play or to hold. And they think they can show all that glitters is gold. And they don't care to go where you go, 'cause they know you're insane, when you change to the Uptown Train'.

By 3.30, after a second verse and chorus, the vocals are over. Piano and bass play a syncopated, low register melody with Houghton marking time, before building up in volume and pitch to an instrumental reprise of the main themes. This gives Jackson a chance to display his blues and jazz piano skills to great effect, the track coming to a close with a drawn-out coda and drum roll.

## 'King Pleasure Time' (2.47)

Another driving rocker, 'King Pleasure Time' could be a further example of Punk Piano (ok, it's a 'thing' now as it's been capitalised) with Jackson hammering away at the ivories in best Jerry Lee Lewis style in this would-be anthem for hedonists everywhere. In the best (Piano) Punk tradition it's brief, sharp, and to the point.

Jackson's vocals are treated to some 'slap-back' delay, and Maby's busy bass line is well forward in the mix, whilst Houghton thrashes his drums with glee. The chorus is another earworm; 'It's King Pleasure time, so show respect, get on your knees, you can't reject his right to please', with backing vocals adding further weight. An instrumental section (1.32-2.08) has a bass solo over a solid piano and drum backing, and another catchy vocal refrain. A third verse and chorus bring the shortest song on the album to a sudden close.

Like 'Citizen Sane' before it, 'King Pleasure Time' is another song which would have been further enhanced by an overdriven electric guitar.

## 'Solo (So Low)' (5.55)

Appropriately enough, this slow ballad features just Jackson and his piano.

The introduction is the underlying arpeggiated chord progression for the bridge section and is a very pretty, harmonically interesting section. Without wishing to bore the reader unfamiliar, or disinterested, in the construction of music, it begins in G minor moving through F major into B flat minor. This 'minor third' uplift modulates to D flat minor, E minor, G minor (again), finally coming to rest on a Bb minor an octave higher than before, and then descending into D minor for the verse.

Jackson's morose lyrics are sung over a pattern of two bars in 4/4 time, and a bar in 2/4 time. This gives the music a stop/start feel, never quite settling but simultaneously fitting the song's downbeat mood. Similarly, the underlying chord sequence (D minor/Eb minor, second inversion) is interesting and dark of hue. One of Jackson's finer vocal moments occurs in the second verse; 'So now to dine, on three stale crackers and a fifth of gin. And say you're fine, feeling like something like that the dog dragged in'. His voice sounds just as good as the piano at this juncture, full and involving.

The previously steady tempo becomes more rubato for the bridge section, gathering pace towards its conclusion; 'Oh, one has to laugh, still safe and warm, with peace of mind after storms'. The arpeggios descend and the tempo tightens for the third verse, which has another spectacular moment (3.06-3.25); 'Scared to find someone in the mirror who you can't recall. Pale and lined, talking to himself and saying, 'Fuck 'em all''.

Another bridge section leads into an instrumental section over the verse chords with Jackson's plaintive melody as good a musical depiction of depression as you will find. At times his solo recalls the series of 'Gymnopedies' compositions by Eric Satie in its sparseness. A further bridge ('Though one gets to play with no referee, peace at last guaranteed') brings the song to an unexpected end, concluding on a counter intuitive chord of A major.

'Solo (So Low)' is a stunning example of the combined emotive power of a skilled songwriter and his chosen instrument, the spaces around the notes and the effortless delivery making this composition something very special indeed.

## 'Rush Across the Road' (5.21)

The mood changes completely for 'Rush Across the Road'; it's light, airy, and positive. The opening line ('Of all the streets in the world, you walk down this one') recalls the famous quotation from the 1942 film *Casablanca*; 'Of all the gin joints in all the towns in all the world, she walks into mine.' Speaking about the song in the accompanying DVD Jackson said:

The whole thing takes place in one moment ... where someone just spots someone on the street they hadn't seen for years, and all the things that go through their head in that moment. Should I rush across the road and grab them and say 'hey, it's me', or not? That song started with the title actually. I seem to remember being on a street in London, and thinking like I'd better rush across the road, and thinking 'That's kinda nice'. The next thing it was going round in my head, complete with the melody of the chorus. I think one of the themes of this record is losing love and finding love again.

The chorus is joyous, melodic, and memorable, and the bridge (2.15-2.47) is even better. Maby has a bass solo which follows, initially, the verse melody before developing and then moving into the third verse; 'Funny how the blink of an eye can last forever, and how we think ourselves dry when it's now or never…'.

The song comes to a false ending at 4.19, before the bridge section is reprised as an instrumental coda for the remaining minute of the song, as it fades away.

## 'Good Bad Boy' (3.18)

This is a much faster, intense and yet still intensely melodic number, with Maby surely wearing his fingers out in his driving accompaniment. Houghton is similarly busy with rapid drum patterns sounding like gunfire in the background.

Jackson is back in sardonic mode playing the part of the agent or manager manipulating a young male and his image for his perceived audience; 'We got it, we're on it, and we can write you like a sonnet, but you can't fight us if you want it'. The chorus ('Get into line and be a good bad boy') is niftily harmonised, whilst the bridge section ('You're our kind of rebel, it's your kind of time, cause everyone gets one chance') twists the lyrical knife still deeper.

The instrumental section (1.43-2.12) takes the listener into unexpected territory. The first 16 bars are a piano and bass duet playing a melody with a Far Eastern flavour, with the remaining ten bars moving through several keys with a jazz-rock feel.

A further bridge and chorus ushers in a reprise of the introduction, this time with just the piano playing, and, at 2.42, the refrain is sung repeatedly with increasing urgency and vocal harmonisation. The rhythm section power in for the final repeats before the song comes to an unusual close with a four whole tone arpeggio resting over a bass B flat.

## 'A Place in The Rain' (5.20)

The album's closer has a more relaxed feel with a 6/8 time signature and restrained contributions from Maby and Houghton. Jackson asserts on the accompanying DVD that he believes his ability as a lyricist is beginning to grow to match his gifts as a musician. This is given plenty of scope here, examples including; 'Turn off the billboards that scream through the night, and dream the policemen to hell', 'Close down the churches and pray to the whores, lay down and then close your eyes', and 'Burn all the papers and burn all the wood, burn what we can't understand'.

The chorus is uplifting, supremely tuneful and just another fine example of what three instruments and a voice are capable of, given the right material; 'It's amazing what comes into view as we're finally breaking the chains. When the temperature rises we'll go to our place in the rain'. Yet again, Jackson's vocal phrasing and tone are exceptional.

An instrumental interlude (2.14-2.24) changes the musical direction briefly before the third set of verses. The third chorus has a nice reference back to an earlier song; 'It's amazing what crazy can do, when every good citizen's sane...'. Following a short instrumental passage, the final chorus ('It's amazing what comes into view *when you just connect your heart back to your brain*, when heaven's a desert we'll go to our place in the rain') has a greater urgency to it with a higher melody for the italicised lyrics.

The song concludes with the main vocal refrain played on piano. Bass and drums drop out and solo piano brings the song to a close, with the sound of falling rain filling the last 30 seconds of the track.

# The Duke

Personnel:

Joe Jackson: keyboards, programming, stylophone, vocals, synth bass, synth guitar, accordion, tom-tom, melodica, vibraphone
Steve Vai: guitar
Kris Ingram Lanzaro: synths, programming
Sussan Deyhim: vocals
Vinnie Zummo: guitars, harmonica
Regina Carter: violin
Mary Rowell: violin
Cornelius Dufallo: violin
Ralph Farris: viola
Dorothy Lawson: cello
Christian McBride: bass guitar, acoustic bass
Ahmir Questlove Thompson: drums
Sue Hadjopoulos; congas, bongos
Tony Aiello: piccolo
Damon Bryson: sousaphone
Sharon Jones: vocals
Kirk Douglas: guitar
Lilian Vieira: vocals and Portuguese translation
Stefan Kruger: drums, percussion, programming
Stefan Schmid: synths, programming
Iggy Pop: vocals
Stefan Schmid: synths, programming
Papa Jo Jones: voice and drum samples
Recorded and mixed at Avatar, New York City
Produced by Joe Jackson
Engineer and Mix: Elliot Scheiner
Assistant engineer: Akihiro Nishimura
All arrangements by Joe Jackson
Released: June 2012 on Edel (Europe)
Released: June 2012 on Razor & Tie (USA)
Highest chart position UK: Did not chart, USA: 93

Following *Rain* Jackson issued another live album, *Live Music, Europe 2010*, musing on his website:

> The trio which made *Rain* (me plus Graham Maby and Dave Houghton) turned out to be my most enduring touring band, and we had a lot of fun on the road for a few years. We went to places I never thought I'd get to, like Israel, Turkey, Mexico and South Africa, and I think this album is a good representation of what we did and is probably my favourite of my live albums.

The tracks were:
'Tomorrow's World', 'Another World', 'Still Alive', 'Chinatown', 'Sunday Papers', 'Cancer', 'Girl', 'Inbetweenies', 'Scary Monsters', 'Got the Time', 'Steppin' Out', 'A Slow Song'.

The last time Jackson released a 'covers' album was, of course, 1981's *Jumpin' Jive*. With his eighteenth studio outing the seemingly ever-restless songwriter took yet another musical diversion, this time with an album dedicated to the American composer, pianist, bandleader, and jazz icon, Duke Ellington, born Edward Kennedy Ellington (1899-1974). Whereas *Jumpin' Jive* contained new versions of old tunes which were faithful in instrumentation and interpretation to the originals, the same cannot be said of *The Duke*. Despite being a huge fan of Ellington Jackson didn't want his tribute to follow the standard, reverential approach. Instead, he filtered Ellington's classic tunes through unexpected rhythms, new arrangements, and unusual musical pairings. Writing in the CD booklet Jackson explained how his approach to reinterpreting Ellington's compositions was inspired by the man himself:

> Nothing is sacred, and anything can be re-arranged and reinvented. The only thing I tried to avoid was imitating or competing with the master. That's why there are no horns in the arrangements. I cheated a bit on 'Rockin' in Rhythm' with a piccolo and a sousaphone, but Ellington at least never used either instrument. By merging songs together into medleys I've managed to cram 15 Ellington tunes into ten tracks. I also felt that those tunes were strong enough with grooves that Ellington didn't live long enough to even imagine... basically, whenever I saw an untravelled path opening up in front of me I took it. God knows what Duke would have thought of all this, but I like to think he would at least have been amused. I'll never know, of course, but I do know that he is one of the Immortals, and nothing I do to his music, however good or bad, is going to change that. I found this idea liberating; ironically, I could be totally irreverent towards music which I revere. I've been wanting to do this for years and it's been a hell of a lot of fun.

*The Duke* is a wide-ranging and (mostly) entertaining experience. Jackson's arrangements of Ellington's songs are inventive and unpredictable with some tracks having echoes of previous albums (the textures of *Night and Day*, *Night and Day II* and *Heaven & Hell* are immediately identifiable). Elsewhere most of the new versions stand up well as individual and independent interpretations of the source material with imagination, creativity, and excellent musicianship.

Ellington once famously said there are only two kinds of music; good and bad. What would he have made of his own compositions being transported into entirely different sound worlds from the one he inhabited? As Jackson says, hopefully, it would bring a smile to his face.

## 'Isfahan' (5.03) (Ellington/Strayhorn)

Named after the city in Iran and first released on Ellington's 1967 album *The Far East Suite*, Jackson's arrangement ups the tempo and dramatically widens the instrumentation, dispensing with the omnipresent alto saxophone of the original.

Opening with a fade in of percussion (to which a lot of reverberation has been added in the studio), a wash of synthesiser strings ushers in the famous melody played in octaves on the piano. So far, so much muzak d'elevator, until at 1.57 where Vai takes over the melody with his lightly distorted guitar sound.

Renowned amongst rock guitarists the world over as one of the instrument's most gifted and individual exponents, Vai significantly dials back the sonic flash and plays Ellington's music with great control and feeling. His phrasing and dynamics allow the melody to shine through, with subtle delays adding much to the ambience. He increases the amount of drive in his tone at 2.24 for the gorgeous soaring development of the main theme, the sound then relaxing back for the conclusion of the section.

Jackson and Vai play off each other to great effect (2.52-3.19) before the guitarist takes the main melody again, reprising the climax at 3.45 before moving into a coda section. Here the initial motif is played at a higher octave before an elegant fretboard flourish brings the piece to a natural end. The final guitar arpeggio is treated with endless repeats and this blends in with the urgent hi-hat and percussion rhythm of the next track...

## 'Caravan' (6.01) (Ellington/Tizol/Mills)

First released in 1936 and subsequently featuring in the soundtracks of the crime caper *Ocean's Eleven* (2001), and *Whiplash* (2014), 'Caravan''s famous, sinewy melody has transformed it, like 'Isfahan', over time into a jazz standard.

In the CD booklet Jackson notes that, despite his obvious artistic abilities, Ellington was no wordsmith. Some of his lyrics were 'so awful' that Jackson encouraged vocalist Sussan Deyhim to translate the composer's words into Farsi (her mother tongue) for this interpretation. 'I'm pretty sure they've greatly improved on the originals' Jackson surmises.

*Night And Day* II style percussion summons in a funky bass line with drums joining in at a faster tempo than the original. Further funk is forthcoming with Zummo's syncopated electric guitar rhythm. Sustained synth strings add to the mix and, in the background, a highly rhythmic violin, viola, and cello ostinato recall the textures of *Heaven & Hell*.

At 1.55 Zummo's heavily distorted guitar takes the main theme and twists it around with savage string bends and plenty of vibrato. The secondary melody is played by Jackson on the Stylophone. This is a handheld simplistic synthesiser, which gives a very cheesy sounding organ, reminiscent of the 1960's children's 'Sci-Fi' shows, of which 'Joe 90' would be the most appropriate example. Zummo returns playing the melody an octave higher.

The introduction is reprised briefly before Deyhim's breathy, close-miked vocals. A heavy, distorted guitar chord leads to a quieter section with percussion, synth strings, bass, and the *Heaven & Hell* string sound building gradually in intensity. Deyhim reprises the secondary and initial melodies before the song comes to an abrupt end on a rising semi-quaver tune.

### 'I'm Beginning To See The Light' (Ellington) / 'Take The 'A' Train (Strayhorn) / 'Cotton Tail' (Ellington) (3.34)

McBride's descending bass line opens this trio, and it would have been good to hear more of his talents in the later instrumental sections of the song. Another track with a decidedly funky feel, 'I'm Beginning to See the Light' is the first to feature Jackson's distinctive singing. The laid-back drumming and prominent acoustic bass lines add a bluesy flavour to the mix, and Carter plays an excellent, lilting violin line as the music transitions into 'Take The 'A' Train' (1.40) where she excels with a soaring interpretation of the main melody.

This continues into the much stronger tune that is 'Cotton Tail' (2.20) as guitar and keyboards join in unison, with phrases being traded between the instruments. At 2.59 Jackson returns with 'I'm Beginning to See the Light' which becomes the coda to the medley. The song concludes, unusually, with a final chord on the first beat of the bar followed by three crochet bass drumbeats. This leaves the listener anticipating a 'Big Band' style ending, which never comes.

Whilst using 'Take The 'A' Train' and 'Cotton Tail' as instrumental interludes within 'I'm Beginning to See the Light', the overall effect is one of trying to put too much into a single piece without giving enough room for the strong melodies and arrangements to fully develop. If the 'A Train' hadn't been taken, and there was more 'Cotton Tail' this medley would be stronger as a result.

### 'Mood Indigo' (4.04) (Ellington/Mills/Bigard)

A slow, bluesy 30-second introduction of violin and accordion leads into Jackson's vocal, with drums, bass and electric guitar as backing. Jackson clearly relishes Ellington's languid melodic phrases, and his voice is treated with plenty of moody reverberation.

At 1.19 there is an unexpected left hand turn into an instrumental with the cello taking the tune over a pizzicato plucked string violin accompaniment. At 2.06 the rhythm section returns with Zummo going full Sixties in his solo before Carter's violin takes over the balance of the melody.

Jackson's laconic voice returns with interjections on the violin as the song glides its dreamy way to a close. The introduction is reprised as a coda with some pretty guitar and cymbal fills in the final few bars.

### 'Rockin' In Rhythm' (3.28) (Ellington)

Drums, sousaphone and a joyous melody played on piccolo and keyboards can't help but bring a smile to the face when listening to this up-tempo, syncopated instrumental. It's all a lot of fun, with plenty of bright piano flurries amongst the musical melee. After the second pass through the main melodies a new section is heard (1.43-2.28) which features rising sustained synth chords over a jungle style drum rhythm, and more piano pyrotechnics. The opening tunes are reprised with a slowed-down bluesy coda which finishes on some held jazzy chords and a flourish of cymbals.

### 'I Ain't Got Nothin' But The Blues' (Ellington/George) / 'Do Nothin' 'Til You Hear From Me' (Ellington/Russell) (5.14)

'Ladies and Gentlemen, will you please welcome... Steely Dan'. Well, obviously not, but the drum groove and off-beat rhythm guitar suggest that Jackson may have been listening to Becker and Fagen.

Sharon Jones gives a fantastic, soulful interpretation of the lyrics for the half-time feel of the verses. The original feel is picked up for the bridge, reverting to half time for the remaining verse. A bluesy piano solo over the guitar, bass, and drums rhythm suddenly changes course at 1.45 into a solo piano section.

Here Jackson takes 'Do Nothin' 'Til You Hear from Me' and strips it right down to its piano-only foundations. Dispensing with the vocals of the original recording, the 'verse' melody is played through three times, with additional instruments joining the texture; melodica, vibraphone, keyboards, bass and drums adding to the late-night cocktail bar feel.

At 2.58 we're back in 'Dan-Land' with an organ taking the place of Jackson's vocals, before the singer returns for the final verse and bridge. The groove keeps powering along with no 'half time' diversions, until the final verse. A piano solo forms the coda with Carter's bluesy asides as the song fades away.

### 'I Got It Bad (And That Ain't Good)' (4.48) (Ellington/Webster)

A beautiful counterpoint quartet of violins, viola and cello brings *Heaven & Hell* to mind again, and acts as an introduction to this slow-moving song which is supported by percussion. Jackson savours every word and note of Ellington's melody, Zummo blows a moody harmonica solo (2.20-3.07), and the whole arrangement is pleasantly relaxing. For the final section the percussion disappears just leaving the string quartet providing the backing.

This absence improves the arrangement, and it would be interesting to hear a version where the percussion is entirely absent, leaving the interweaving instrumental lines and harmony to support Jackson's earnest vocals.

### 'Perdido' (Tizol/Lenk/Drake) / 'Satin Doll' (Ellington/Mercer/Strayhorn) (4.49)

The *Night and Day* feel continues with Hadjopoulos' percussion in this medium tempo, sparse and lightweight arrangement. At Jackson's request, Lilian Vieira sings this song in her first language, Portuguese, with Zummo's strummed acoustic guitar giving the song a distinctly 'vibe d'hotel foyer' feel. Fortunately, things become briefly more interesting for his distorted guitar solo (1.18-1.33).

At 2.01 the band slide into 'Satin Doll' with Zummo's guitar enjoying prominence. This quickly turns into a stride piano solo at a slower tempo (2.45-3.55) which moves into waltz time (3.38-3.45) before returning to 4/4 and slowing with some sustained chords. This ushers in a repeat of 'Perdido' complete with Vieira's delightful vocals, the song coming to a sudden second beat end.

### 'The Mooche' (Ellington/Miley) / 'Black And Tan Fantasy' (Ellington) (5.26)

The sleazy feel of the original is replicated with Steve Vai providing biting, harmonised, sustained lead guitar lines in between which some heavily distorted lower register wah-wah pedal abuse sounds like a grumpy dog having a bad day.

This opening texture (0.08-0.58) quickly changes musical course into a quaint sounding section; the string section plays the main melody over acoustic bass and light shaker. The introduction is reprised at 1.23 with Vai's guitars and pissed-off pooch pedal making a re-appearance. At 2.05 the cello takes over with 'Black And Tan Fantasy' against a light reggae style accompaniment. This section reminds me of Andrew Lloyd-Webber's album *Variations* (1978) which did for Paganini (1782-1840) what Jackson is doing for Ellington.

At 2.30, Vai unleashes his miserable mutt again for a master class demonstration of the range of expression an electric guitar is capable of in the right (and left) hands. At 3.03 there is another unexpected change with an organ solo played out over light drumming, which then moves into accordion and strings in a syncopated section (3.29-4.03)

The 'Mooche' is then reprised as the coda to this arrangement, the music concluding with the familiar phrases from Frederick Chopin's 'Funeral March' (from the third movement of his second piano sonata), culminating in an upward run of notes from Vai, and a piano arpeggio from Jackson.

### 'It Don't Mean A Thing (If It Ain't Got That Swing)' (5.08) (Ellington/Mills)

'It Don't Mean A Thing...' is probably Ellington's most famous song. On this album, it's the one that gets the most bizarre treatment.

A mixture of electronica, spoken word, and – sometimes – the actual song, Jackson opens proceedings over a brisk rhythm section with the song's familiar introduction ('What good is melody? What good is music?') gets a more conventional (for this album) opening.

Then the weirdness begins... keyboard motifs, jazz drumming, walking bass lines, spoken word excerpts, and then we're into a more conventional arrangement with a vibraphone taking the melody. A brief syncopated section acts as an introduction for Iggy Pop's vocal contribution which, to be kind, is not perhaps his finest work. In the background 'Doo-Wah' vocals add class to proceedings.

At 2.54 an instrumental section begins with Carter playing some glorious jazz violin phrases before Zummo goes full 'Hot Club' with his frenetic acoustic Django Reinhardt impression. Four bars of acoustic bass lead to violin and guitar battling for sonic space before Jackson returns. Echoed 'doo-wah' vocals, more electronica, bass and drums, and spoken words lead this very strange interpretation to a fade.

# Fast Forward

Personnel:
Joe Jackson: vocals, keyboards, programming
New York:
Bill Frisell: guitar
Brian Blade: drums
Graham Maby: bass, vocals
Regina Carter: violin
Recorded by Patrick Dillett at his studio, New York
Amsterdam:
Stefan Kruger: drums
Aram Kersbergen: acoustic and electric bass
Claus Tofft: percussion
Guido Nijs: saxophones
Jan van Duikeren: trumpet
Borika van den Booren: first violin
Michael Waterman: second violin
Edith van Moergastel: viola
Benedikt Enzler: cello
Jan Van Duikeren: trumpet
Mitchell Sink: vocals
Recorded by Kasper Frenkel at Electric Monkey, Amsterdam
Berlin:
Greg Cohen: acoustic bass
Earl Harvin: drums, percussion
Dirk Berger: guitar
Markus Ehrlich: tenor saxophone
Dima Bondarev: trumpet
Recorded by Tobias Lehmann at Teldex, and Peter Schmidt at Ballsaal, Berlin
New Orleans:
Stanton Moore: drums, percussion
Donald Harrison, Jr: alto saxophone
Robert Mercurio: bass guitar
Jeffrey Raines: guitar
Sam 'Big Sam' Williams: trombone
John Michael Bradford: trumpet
Recorded by Misha Kachkachishvili at Esplanade, New Orleans
Pre-production by Joe Jackson and Michael Tibes at Fuzz Factory, Berlin
Produced and arranged by Joe Jackson
Mixed by Patrick Dillett
Mastered by Ted Jensen at Sterling Sound, New York
All songs by Joe Jackson except 'See No Evil' (Verlaine), and 'Good Bye Jonny' (Kreuder/Beckman)

Released: October 2015 on Caroline Records
Highest chart position UK: 168, USA: 45

*Fast Forward* grew from plans for a series of four-track EPs, each relating to a specific city (New York, Amsterdam, Berlin, and New Orleans), with a different set of musicians playing on each group of songs. Eventually, the EPs were combined into a 'double-studio' album.

For his 2015 album, the seemingly ever-restless Jackson continued to mine his deep vein of memorable songs. Lyrically, he is still analysing the complexities of life in the modern world, combined with a yearning for connection, and that is not meant as a criticism. Exploring the human condition is a never-ending task for any artist; there are always new impressions to be made, and, yet again, Jackson produces several thought-provoking lines and circumstances. The album is an experiment that works well and shows Jackson's musical curiosity is as strong as ever.

## 'Fast Forward' (6.03)
The title track is a medium-paced number which never stands still musically and is Jackson's 'wordiest' song to date. Opening in B major with a subtle drum machine and gentle piano, the song modulates into D major, then F major, followed by Ab major and returning to F major again for the first lyrics. Instantly familiar as a Jackson composition as soon as his distinctive vocals begin, this is also a fresh style of composition, never coming to rest for too long.

As constantly shifting as its composer, 'Fast Forward' is a wishful song, hoping that at some time in the future 'people will be happy instead of getting dumber and getting scareder all the time'. Jackson accurately sums up the situation for people living at the extremes; 'either miserable with millions or dying for a dime, desperate to live forever or lucky to live at all'.

Intensely melodic, 'Fast Forward' revolves through the four-modulation pattern until the bridge section (2.53-3.25). Here Jackson imagines the moon looking down on us 'watching us as fools and geniuses rush in, and you and me age disgracefully and have way too much fun'. The chord sequence changes again (B minor, G sharp minor 7, G major 7, E major), and this is repeated for Carter's haunting violin solo (3.26-4.05).

The piano introduction is then reprised, and we're into the final third of the song. The hypnotic pace and ceaseless chord manoeuvrings continue, but the song never becomes boring, with Jackson striking an optimistic tone with the lines 'We can make the future, make it every bit as clear, make a friendly *Star Trek* universe, cause everything's allowed', because 'the only place that's seriously strange to be is here, and the only time that's maddeningly mysterious is now'.

'Fast Forward' was never going to have a definitive end, and the song fades away after a repeat of the catchy refrain 'Not going back to the Age of Gold or the Age of Sin, fast forward till I understand the age I'm in' which is a perfect summation of the song's lyrics.

## 'If It Wasn't for You' (3.37)

Track two is a more up-tempo tune that deals with the ebb and flow of relationships, and the rationalisations which are made to justify failings. Sound-wise there are some charmingly chorused guitar arpeggios in the background, with a busy drum rhythm and a prominent bass, especially in the very catchy chorus.

The song's title features as the first line of each verse; Jackson's song character muses that if it wasn't for 'you' everything needn't be 'such a fuss', and that he could 'do better sleeping better at night'. For the third verse, however, he turns the criticism on himself; 'If it wasn't for me I guess, you could be someone better by now.' The chorus goes into double-time; 'You can be anything, a slave or a master, any joker or any king can be a sad bastard'. His tone and inflection on this latter line is quintessential Jackson, edgy and direct. He follows this with another nice 'role reversal' line in the refrain 'And I'd be one too, if it wasn't for you'.

After the second chorus, the instrumental section (2.17-2.51) is divided between Jackson's trademark high octave piano and a melodic, slightly distorted guitar solo, which has echoes of Steely Dan's early work to it. A reprise of the first chorus, with repeated refrains, leads into a brief coda section, which consists of rising chords leading to a definitive end.

## 'See No Evil' (4.08)

Compared to the gritty original, complete with Wishbone Ash-esque harmony guitars, Jackson's take on this 1977 song from *Marquee Moon*, the debut album by New York-based band Television, is less aggressive and more stylised. Does this polishing add anything to this excellent song?

Structurally identical to the earlier version, Jackson's cover version is taken at a slightly slower tempo, with a sparser musical texture; there is more sound around the music. If you were unaware, you'd never know that 'See No Evil' wasn't a Joe Jackson composition as there are some lines that sound just like his lyrical style; 'I understand your destructive urges, it seems so perfect' and 'I get your point, you're so sharp, getting good reactions with your Bebo talk'.

Following the second chorus, there is a truly dreadful, sixteen bar guitar solo (1.49-2.17). Part wah-wah pedal abuse, part heavily flanged dissonance, and part 'I've just passed my Grade Five exam' level of fretboard invention, it is the sonic low point of the album.

So, a great track gets a reasonable makeover, but why? The original is superior, Jackson (a master of transforming his own recorded material into significantly different live variations) does very little of note to the composition. It isn't as if he's exactly lacking in material, as the fourteen new songs on this new album illustrate. So, again, why is it here? Discuss.

## 'Kings Of the City' (5.23)
In a 2016 interview with *Classic Pop* Jackson described this as:

> ...a bittersweet song about people who grew up in the middle of nowhere, moving to a big city. They've gained some things and lost others; as the chorus says 'They have the bright lights but they can't see the stars anymore.

The New York section concludes with this nostalgic, bittersweet, and utterly beguiling ballad. A gorgeous-sounding electric piano, low key drum machine and acoustic piano provide the hypnotic backing to Jackson's elegiac vocals. Lyrically it's a 'then and now' comparison piece that examines how our attitudes change as we get older, moving from youthful expectations to the adult realization that 'nobody's perfect, and everything's real'.

There is an autobiographical element to the lyrics; 'We were brought up in a boring town, watching our feet sink into the ground', and now, living on 'top of a tower of steel' Jackson 'listens to sirens and neighbours who fight', ruefully reflecting that 'we don't see the stars anymore'. 'Kings Of the City' builds magnificently into its anthemic chorus, with its harmonised backing vocals and a classy level of reverb added to the sound.

An understated instrumental section (3.31-3.34) features a restrained, melodic guitar solo, with the song coming to a false ending before Jackson rouses the music again ('Come with me up on the roof tonight, you know we'll be kings of the city and look at the lights') into a final chorus. The track fades over the repeated 'We don't see the stars' refrain with some pretty guitar fills decorating the soundscape.

## 'A Little Smile' (4.00)
The 'Amsterdam EP' opens with this up-beat, radio-friendly track. Lyrically this describes a situation after a disagreement between a couple, with an attempt to lighten the atmosphere, although, as Jackson wryly notes, 'these things are hit and miss'.

Driven along by relentless drums and a throbbing bass 'A Little Smile' is initially melodically engaging and harmless enough, but fortunately grinds up a gear at 1.01 with the chorus; 'Someone else might come with another plan, someone else could be twice as smart. I'll put one foot in front of the other, no other way I can make a start'. Syncopated and high in energy, this is the standout section of the song, although Jackson hits lyrical gold in the next verse with the line 'You can't ask for more than something that won't grow old'.

A second chorus leads into an instrumental section which blends violins playing the vocal melody line with Jackson's piano in an attractive duet. The eight-bar chorus is extended by the addition of an extra four bars of music after each four-bar vocal phrase. This idea is repeated, and at 3.38 there is a more relaxed coda section, which comes to a clumsy rehearsal-style ending.

## 'Far Away' (4.03)

In an interview with *Salon.com* in September 2015, Jackson explained the song's origins:

> 'Far Away' started its life as a song for 'Stoker'. In the show, it's sung by Stoker as a young boy. And the music is substantially the same, but since I thought that song may never see the light of day, I rewrote it and then changed the lyrics and took it in a different direction and it becomes about…, well I like the idea of how in a movie sometimes you'll see a character as a child, and then time passes, and you see the same character as an adult. And I thought it'd be cool to do that in a song.

'Far Away' is, ahem, far and away, the most intriguing song on *Fast Forward*. A slow-moving composition in 6/4 time with a strong string presence, the central motif is a rising arpeggio sequence of a repeated F sharp minor, B7 (first inversion), C sharp 7 (also first inversion) chord sequence, which is played with a synthesised harp sound.

This hypnotic effect continues for the first half of the verse, which, unexpectedly, introduces Jackson as a child, his thoughts sung by fourteen-year-old Mitchell Sink; 'It's me and me alone, against the night, so easy to be scared without the light'. The young Jackson listens to the trains which, in the chorus, will take him 'far away from England, my dreams and me'.

It's a song of two halves; the second part modulates up a semitone as the present-day Jackson takes over the vocals; 'It's me and me alone, against the world, so far from all the cares of boys and girls'. In the here and now he hears the planes that flew him 'far away from England, my dreams and me'.

From 3.02 the verse arpeggio continues, being constantly repeated as the music fades away in this track which takes the yearning and excitement of youth, and neatly juxtaposes it with the wisdom and maturity of adulthood.

## 'So You Say' (2.52)

A medium paced, pleasant enough little ode, 'So You Say' has too much 'muzak d'hotel lobby' about it to maintain listening interest. It's a light jazz number with syncopated rhythms and percussion in the background. It's not too much of a stretch to imagine it being an offcut from *Night and Day*.

The chorus ('And I thought I knew what went on in my heart, till you taught me I would never have been smart enough to leave you') is better with a stronger vocal melody, but then we're back in Reception with an uninvolving piano-led instrumental. A further chorus leads into the final verses, and the shortest song on the album comes to a clumsy, 'demo'-like sudden ending.

## 'Poor Thing' (3.32)

Set in a rolling 6/8-time signature, 'Poor Thing' is, fortunately, stronger. Again it's mid-paced, but the vocal melody is superior, and the welcome addition of the brass players adds a sense of power and purpose to the song's chorus.

Lyrically this, the final contribution from Holland, takes a wide-angle lens view of humanity, focussing on one particular individual A younger Jackson might have taken the 'glass half empty' option lyrically; here, he is merely the observer of someone for whom 'everything's tragic today, and your life's a mess', before concluding that 'maybe you like it that way, that could make sense, I guess'. He takes a more positive stance in the final verse; 'There must still be a few million chances that just a few things could still turn out okay, so on we go'.

There's an interesting section (1.08-1.15) featuring a jazzy vibraphone playing a rapid semi-quaver descending melody after the first chorus. After the second chorus, the instrumental section is handed over to the horns before a final chorus. The jazzy vibraphone solo makes a reappearance as a brief coda.

## 'Junkie Diva' (5.39)
In an interview with the *Pittsburgh Post-Gazette* in October 2015 Jackson said:

Everyone thinks it's about Amy Winehouse! Well, OK. Firstly, it's not about a specific person, it's more about the obsessive fan than about the diva. It's more about the way people project what they see on certain figures, and the way that they live things vicariously through their heroes or idols, and they want to themselves, literally or figuratively. But that's really what the song is about, and as far as who the diva is, when I was writing it, I was thinking about Billie Holiday.

The Berlin segment kicks off with this mid-paced groover which is simplistic in its construction. Driven along by a syncopated electric piano riff 'Junkie Diva' is a welcome return to Jackson's acerbic persona; 'Anything you tell me, it's got to be real, can you tell me how I feel', and, in the final verse, 'You didn't get a chance to go on too long. You're even better now you're gone'.

The chorus is excellent; highly melodic and catchy, even if the refrain 'Down, down with the Junkie Diva' does sound very similar to the chorus of 'Dirty Martini' *(Volume 4)*. Jackson gives full rein to his vocal skills, adding just the right amount of sneer to his inflection.

At 3.09, after the second chorus the musical mood changes with an instrumental section which again has the feel of *Night and Day II* about it. In the background, the electric guitar is a welcome addition to the texture, and this track would be even stronger if the guitar was more prominent in the verse and bridge sections. The sound is clean and chiming, some distortion would have broadened the song's effect even more. This section is repeated after the final vocal section, acting as a coda with, strangely, the drum rhythm continuing to a fade as the final chords sustain dies away.

## 'If I Could See Your Face' (4.20)
From the same interview with *Classic Pop* Jackson said:

'If I Could See Your Face' is quite an angry song, but it's the anger of feeling helpless and not being able to understand things. How can radically different cultures exist side by side? I think we have to be more realistic about this as a society. This song came partly out of my observations of the Turkish community in Berlin, and partly a real-life Berlin story, the young Turkish girl who was murdered by her brothers for 'dishonouring the family'. I'm not saying Turks are all going round killing their sisters, it's just an extreme example of a real problem.

The dark mood of 'Junkie Diva' deepens with this deliberately confrontational rocker. The introduction is, however, anything but; an atmospheric sustained synthesiser chord and counterpoint melodies between saxophone and trumpet over a steady hi-hat beat reaches a crescendo 38 seconds in and an angry-sounding, distorted guitar and aggressive drumming take over the soundstage. The underlying chord sequence (moving repeatedly between E minor and F major) creates an appropriately exotic feel, part Spanish, part further Eastern, as Jackson unleashes his excoriating lyrics; 'If I could see your face, the face of the girl behind the veil, I'd ask you if it feels like a guarantee, to keep you down or keep you safe, or just to keep you pale'.

Jackson goes for the throat pointing out how some Islamic practices do not fit in with Western cultural freedoms using the examples of the subjugation of women, and 'honour killings' taking place in Europe. Is the girl behind the burka truly happy and how can he be sure her answer is not forced. The music lifts into a melodic chorus set mainly in G major; 'But respect, respect, respect my culture. We're all part of the human race. Questions, questions, would you answer?'

Amidst this disturbing composition, a 'West-meets-East' instrumental section begins at 2.42 with a church organ synthesiser playing a distinctly Baroque style solo (think any Jon Lord contribution from almost any Deep Purple song) for eight bars, before tripping into a more Eastern flavoured style for four bars. The remaining eight bars reprises the saxophone and trumpet melody from the introduction under the heavy drumming rhythm. This is then repeated as a refrain as the music goes into a fade.

## 'The Blue Time' (5.32)
With its percussive background, strong octave piano presence, and slow tempo 'The Blue Time' has a *Night and Day* feel to it. It is another of Jackson's beautifully evocative ballads with a sound which just shimmers; the degree of reverberation is particularly effective in highlighting Jackson's yearning voice.

The music builds in volume and texture ('And it starts to rain, and blue turns indigo') leading into the instrumental section. The trumpet solo (2.36 - 2.59) conjures up the past glories of 'Body and Soul', and this is followed by a simple yet tasteful guitar solo; both instrumentalists reinterpreting the vocal melodies which have preceded them, creating a dreamlike state. Extremely atmospheric and containing much dynamic control and release the song is another masterpiece of melody, lyric, and consummate skill in arrangement and performance.

## 'Goodbye Jonny' (5.42)

The final song of the Berlin group is a cover of this German Pre-World War Two song and, whilst it's a typical Jackson reinterpretation sung with relish and performed with spirit, the question immediately leaps to mind 'Why have you recorded this?' Given the eclectic range of Jackson's compositional skills, it's easy to imagine (again, if you didn't know better) that Jackson could have written the song. But he didn't. So why is it here?

## 'Neon Rain' (3.35)

And off we now go to New Orleans where, as might be expected, the music is underpinned by a jazzier feel.

The opening song of the section, however, has 'RAWK!' written all the way through it with plenty of percussion, overdriven guitar, and a riotous vocal sound. 'Neon Rain' has elements of glam rock, without sounding like a pastiche, with plenty of attitude, and is a welcome uplift in feel.

Despite its celebratory sound, the lyrics are dark; 'I stepped out in the pouring rain to find a place where they feel my pain', and the entire chorus; 'You don't like me, you don't need me, you won't see me on the other side of town in the neon rain'. Jackson's voice is aggressive throughout, yet never leaving the melody behind, and the backing vocals are the sound of a group of men in 'call-and-response' mode.

From 2.33 (where Jackson gives us his convincing impression of a werewolf) the remainder of the track is an instrumental play-out with the guitar well to the fore. This is a song which could have done with further development; it's over too soon, and more lyrics and some dynamic change would have turned this (for Jackson) headbanging number into something even stronger.

## 'Satellite' (4.24)

A mournful-sounding brass introduction blends into a syncopated, mid-paced track with hints of Steely Dan to it. Guitar and piano have sparse contributions amongst the rhythm, the space around the music helping to focus attention on the lyrics.

'Satellite' deals with infatuation from a fresh perspective, although the opening couplet is less than stellar; 'I remember lying wide awake at night, had to have you by my side to make it right'. Jackson sings this in harmony with himself, his falsetto voice being an octave higher than his usual range. It's an effective trick and gives the song an ambivalent identity: is it male to female, female to male, male to male or female to female?

The chorus is superb, full-blooded, melodic, and memorable, with gorgeous vocal harmonies, and the trumpet providing a sad counterpoint. After the second chorus, there is another lengthy instrumental playout featuring a repeated, simple trumpet harmony phrase against the evocative drum patterns.

## 'Keep on Dreaming' (4.18)

This has an excellent, soulful funk-groove running through it after Jackson's direct voice and piano introduction; 'God must think he's God or something, Lording it over us, seems to like to make us feel ridiculous'. The chorus refrain, ('keep on dreaming till I get it right, even if I never get it right'), is a guaranteed audience sing-along, and this is followed by a short funky, syncopated descending melody into another verse and chorus.

Following the second chorus and refrain, the instrumental is a showcase for Jackson's piano skills where he fuses blues and funk to great effect. At 2.40, the solo is handed over to the alto saxophone for sixteen bars. The play-out section begins at 3.04, with the horns exchanging phrases with Jackson's refrain for a further sixteen bars which is followed by the short funky phrase. The refrain is repeated with brass and saxophone interjections and rather than go for what feels like an obligatory fade the instruments all cut out at 4.13 leaving just the harmonised refrain as a sudden ending.

## 'Ode To Joy' (4.17)

Another heavily percussive number, this one more African than Latin, takes elements of Beethoven's famous tune (more accurately it's the prelude to the fourth movement of Symphony No. 9,) and puts it in a new song setting.

A sustained organ plays over a steady 6/4 time syncopated percussion pattern and Jackson's vocals soar; 'Impossible to see, impossible to show, impossible to verify, impossible to know'. Piano joins the instrumentation as the music grows to a crescendo 'Joy' and Kumpel's distorted guitar plays an excerpt of Beethoven's melody. The song moves into the more uneven 5/4 time for the chorus.

The music quietens back down to percussion then the second verse begins with an identical structure as the first section to another 'Joy'. From 2.20 onwards is an instrumental reprise of what's gone before with some smooth brass soloing. At 3.23 there is a repeated chorus with a sudden silence before the 'Joy', with Kumpel repeating the Beethoven melody to the fade.

# Fool

Personnel:
Joe Jackson: vocals, keyboards, programming
Graham Maby: bass, vocals
Teddy Kumpel: guitar, vocals
Doug Yowell: drums, programming, vocals
Written by Joe Jackson
Recorded at the Tonic Room, Boise, Idaho
Produced by Joe Jackson and Patrick Dillett
Mixed by Patrick Dillett at Reservoir, New York City
Mastered by Greg Calbi, Sterling Sound
Released: January 2019 on Edel AG Records
Highest chart position UK: 13, USA: 25

As part of 'Record Store Day' in 2017 Jackson released the single 'Fools In Love' backed by 'Music To Watch Girls By', which was a previously unreleased live recording made with the *Rain* trio.

With his most recent album, Jackson found himself, whether intentionally or not, turning full circle and returning to the format with which he started his career, a four-piece rock band. *Fool* is also a more concise offering than *Fast Forward*; just eight songs played by the same four musicians as that album. The band had played live together since the release of *Fast Forward*.

The album was the fulfilment of a career-long dream for Jackson; to finish a tour and head straight into the studio with the band firing on all cylinders. On 30 July 2018, his 103-show tour having concluded at The Egyptian Theatre in Boise, Idaho the previous night, Jackson, Maby, Kumpel and Yowell set up to play once again, this time at Tonic Room Studios to commence recording.

## 'Big Black Cloud' (6.02)
In an interview with *Record Collector* in February 2019, Jackson commented on the lyrics of the album opener:

> This one's about fear and paranoia – people seem to be scared of more and more things than they used to be. People in authority have always used fear as a way to legitimise themselves; it's a time-honoured way of ruling people to more or less say, 'The sky is falling, but if you support me, I'll make you safe and keep your children safe.' What we don't hear is people being inspiring; there's more fearmongering than inspiration.

'Big Black Cloud' is one hell of a song. Dark and tense, bordering at times on outright heavy rock, it is a song of epic proportions and sound. Clever alterations in dynamics and texture ensure interest is never lost in the album's second-longest track; the melodies are strong and Jackson sings with power and conviction. Kumpel's guitar is heavily distorted, and the majority of the track has an air of deep foreboding (which is substantially enhanced by the reverberation), from the relentless piano rhythm to the aggressive drums of Doug ('The Thug' as Jackson has amusingly referred to him in concert) Yowell.

The mood only lightens slightly for the chorus; 'Save us from the big black cloud, shout it out, not too loud', only for an overpoweringly heavy sound to kick the door down with the bridge section (2.24-2.56); 'No luck, no money, no sex, no fun. Get on the treadmill and run, run, run, run, run'. There are heavy metal bands who sound less brutal and committed than this.

After a repeat of the bridge section (4.01-4.40), the music quietens considerably with some chiming guitar chords and Jackson's plaintive piano melody fragments leading into an extended fade, as if the band have expended all available effort into the song up to this point and are now exhausted.

## 'Fabulously Absolute' (4.14)

This song harks back to *Look Sharp* and *I'm The Man* with a jaunty, distorted guitar riff that Gary Sanford would be happy to play. Maby's busy bass and Yowell's syncopation drive the song into another powerful chorus. There is a real punkish rake to Jackson's delivery, and only the strength of the melodies prevents this song from turning into a late 1970s thrashy pastiche.

The style changes dramatically for the bridge section (2.17-2.42) lurching unexpectedly into full-on prog rock, complete with rapid rising and falling synthesiser melodies, over which Jackson continues to spit bile; 'I'm a bigot and a boob, I'm a racist and a rube, I'm a hater and a hick, I'm a sinner and I'm sick!'

'Fabulously Absolute' is a first-class piece of riotous fun, full of angst and tension, and yet always melodic and lyrically clever. It is further proof that despite all the musical twists and turns in Jackson's long and very varied career he remains a songwriter with wit, craft, and genuine talent.

## 'Dave' (5.04)

This is a slower-paced song, dominated by the piano and Jackson's close-miked vocal. Another highly melodic number which has echoes of The Beatles and The Kinks about it in its story-telling imagery, the focus shifts from the titular character in the chorus to 'You and me' who 'just keep on rushing round the world to chase the perfect crime. Could it be that while we're rushing round the world we're wasting all our time?'

There is a beautiful, lightly distorted guitar solo from Kumpel which leads into a quieter third verse as Jackson savages a world seemingly over-populated by 'Daves'; 'Dave lies in his grave, under the hill, somebody took his place with the same face, whistles the same tone-deaf tune, works until noon, howls at the moon, maybe he'll call in sick, head like a brick, says you can just call him Dave'.

The anticipated fade after repeated refrains of 'Wasting all our time' doesn't materialise, the song coming to rest on a non-tonic chord, leaving Jackson's fundamental question unanswered; are you better off staying in one place, or travelling all the time?

## 'Strange Land' (5.42)

In an interview with *De Volkskrant* (a Dutch publication) in January 2019 Jackson said:

> That's partly about New York. When I lived there in the '80s I loved it. I still visit the city regularly, but now it feels so different. Everything that was familiar to me is gone. There are other things in its place that I don't know at all. That is why I often feel disconnected from my surroundings, a wandering ghost...

'Strange Land' is an even slower-paced song, laced with atmospheric piano and sustained guitar over a relentless rim-shot rhythm with plenty of reverb added to create an unsettling mood, with more excellent lyrics; 'I study the lines on the map, and the lines on my face, am I out of time or out of place?' Kumpel is a strong contributor here with some well-placed and thoughtful melodic lines. Jackson's lyrics are as evocative as his vocals; 'Rainy Sunday afternoon, looking for a toast, all the whisky's Japanese, the bars are full of ghosts, here in the City of Lights I'm looking for a cave. Am I a soul who can't be saved?'

Melancholic guitar and Jackson's fragmented piano solo ensure that a trance-like mood dominates the song; the dynamic structure doesn't alter substantially and, whilst this isn't one of Jackson's more memorable compositions, what it does it does extremely well. Inevitably the song goes into a long fade, drifting away to nothing.

## 'Friend Better' (4.51)

After two introspective tracks Jackson brightens the mood with 'Friend Better'; the opening of which recalls 'Down To London' (*Blaze Of Glory*) with its syncopated piano riff and distinctive tambourine. The chorus is another belter, enhanced by strong backing vocals, whilst Kumpel channels his inner Steely Dan with some tasteful fills throughout the song.

The instrumental section (2.02-2.33) has a real earworm of a melody although, weirdly, this is played with an organ tone which sounds out of place. This is repeated after the third verse and chorus, and its strength is reinforced when the majority of the instruments are silent, leaving just the sing-along refrain. Everyone's back on board for the eventual fade of this excellent, radio-friendly song.

## 'Fool' (4.59)

In an interview with *billboard.com* in January 2019, Jackson said:

> I imagine this character, the fool, as the personification of humour. And he's like a superhero. He's got this power to make people laugh, and he's

invulnerable. You can't kill him, and he lives forever. He's never gonna go away, at least I hope not. Every totalitarian regime has tried to suppress humour because tyrants can't bear to be laughed at, but you can't stop it in the end. I think it's one of the most amazing things about human beings.

In the accompanying song lyric booklet is printed, in a small font at the end of this song's words, the following: 'Warning: may contain traces of *Twelfth Night* and *King Lear*'.

Wow, this one is noisy! The faded-in opening recalls the theme from the 1960s television show *Batman*, but with an Oriental guitar tone. Crashing power chords, syncopated drums and the vocals recalling elements of *Beat Crazy* with the treatment of the opening stanzas (a megaphone and plenty of reverb), there is just so much going on in this track. And that's just in the first thirty seconds.

Dispensing with the megaphone, Jackson's next vocals have a 'rock-meets-traditional folk' feel, especially with the backing vocal refrain ('Heigh-ho, the wind and the rain'), and the chorus is another lyrically sharp and musically busy section; 'Fool, kicks off the carnival, wise man goes to church. Fool – fucks up the funeral, no respect, well what did you expect?'. This is followed by another Oriental-tinged instrumental section (1.10-1.30), helped along by a sitar-sounding guitar melody.

## '32 Kisses' (4.28)

The introduction sounds like a distant relative of Pachelbel's famous 'Canon' on amphetamines, but the emergence of the light drums and a delightful, slightly distorted guitar line take us into another melodic goldmine.

'32 Kisses' is another of Jackson's reflective, retrospective numbers (it is a distant cousin, lyrically at least, of 'Chrome' from *Volume 4*) as the first verse deals with the passage of time; 'Another day, another year, another miracle, another tear, another birthday, another card, another memory from so near so far'.

The excellent chorus brings the past into sharp focus with Jackson remembering, 'I saw you grow, I saw it all, from the head of your class to the queen of the stage. Strange I know what I recall is the 32 kisses at the foot of the page'. Here the music has a double-time feel to it without actually changing metre, with Kumpel's guitar mirroring the vocal melody.

The second verse has Jackson recalling his relationship with the protagonist where 'we had a time, a year or five. We had an ending, but we got to be alive'. This rhyme, and indeed idea, is a reprise of 'Still Alive', also from *Volume 4*. After the second chorus, the song performs a weird volte-face, lurching into 3/4 time and taking on the feel of a reprise of 'Goodbye Jonny' from *Fast Forward*. The chords and vocal melody descend, finally coming to rest for the final line; 'The lucky few who get to have a life'.

The song moves back into 4/4 for a repeated first verse after Maby has a well-phrased eight-bar solo. The superb chorus is reprised with Kumpel's guitar melody rising over the chord sequence as the song comes to an uplifting conclusion.

## 'Alchemy' (6.45)

In an interview with *Bremen Zwei*, a German radio station, in January 2019 Jackson said:

> I had a certain atmosphere in mind, and I wanted to do something like I imagined a theme tune for an imaginary James Bond movie or something like this. You know, the opening credits, very lush and kind of old movie music. The song is really about the magic of any kind of art, whatever kind of art moves you, because it refers to movies, to music, to dance. And I really like this idea of the artist being an alchemist who can create magic out of ordinary things.

Alchemy, the medieval forerunner of chemistry, is the transmutation of matter, typically the conversion of base metals into gold, or the search for a universal elixir. Jackson's 'Alchemy' does none of these things. Ironically this long, bossa-nova based ballad originally sounds like it's going to be quite the epic, only to end up as a very dull and uninvolving song.

Musically 'Alchemy' is the sound of muzak in a large, empty restaurant. Probably a 'Harvester'. On a business park. Just outside Milton Keynes. Yes, the song is atmospheric and has a reasonably strong, sinuous central instrumental melody, but the overall effect is dreamlike and not in a good way.

Lyrically it's much better; the first verse depicts a magician doing his disappearing act, the second describes a romantic rendezvous and the third is the best of all; 'Beautiful dancers fly into the air, enchanted by a melody that isn't really there. A savage beast has turned into a man, the curtains close to open on command, Alchemy'.

The mid-section, like '32 Kisses' before it, enters strange territory; a very jazzy chord progression ushers in some perplexing words; 'Thrill – to secrets never told. Taste – the bitter turned to sweet. See – the dross turned into gold. Hear – a B sharp turned to C'. As most musicians know, the notes of B sharp and C are two different names for the same pitch of sound. Perhaps it's one of those joke things. Another pint of overpriced, underachieving lager, anyone? Our special today is the lasagne.

The best part of this song is the beautifully sustained, distorted guitar tone Kumpel employs for his solo section (3.48 – 4.38), where he reprises the main melodic theme with great taste and restraint, but after the third verse, the track drifts off into a long fade leaving a sense of disappointment and underachievement in this, the album's longest song.

# Sing, You Sinners!

In *A Cure For Gravity* Jackson writes approvingly of George Gershwin (1898-1937), the American pianist and composer of 'Rhapsody In Blue' fame as a musician who straddled the pop and classical genres. There are similarities; like Gershwin, Jackson has a restless musical imagination and at times it's hard to believe that the Jackson of 'Is She Really Going Out with Him' is the same man who later served up the deep and challenging complexities of *Heaven & Hell*. Or the writer of the heavily reggae and ska-influenced *Beat Crazy* is the consummate musician who, five years later, gave us the incredible blend of songs that makes up *Body And Soul*. He is all of these, and more.

I've never had the pleasure of meeting Joe Jackson, and, if I had, I wouldn't mention it (I'm not given to name dropping, as I was only saying to the Pope over a beer yesterday). But if I were to meet Jackson I would want to thank him for the range and depth of his talent. His music has enhanced my life, and there are no other artists I can think of who have displayed such a phenomenal talent and stuck resolutely, some might say in certain instances bloody mindedly, to playing exactly what he wants to play. Not for him the 'stuck-in-a-style' rut from which some artists never seem to escape; Jackson is the eternal musical wanderer, led by his own muse and instincts and taking us with him, safe in the knowledge that whatever he produces it will be original, inventive, and written with a rare quality always front and centre; integrity.

By the time you are reading this, Joe Jackson will have undertaken a new world tour with the band which played on *Fool*, and the successful 'Four Decades' Tour of 2019. On his website Jackson promised:

The new show will feature both the full band and a 'mini-set' of Joe solo. The songs will be drawn from Joe's whole career, including some that haven't been heard live in many years. Watch out also for some surprises, including some completely new material. The tour will take the band to some cities Joe has never played or hasn't played for a long time.

We've been dealing with two viruses over the past two years, and the worst – the one we really need to put behind us – is fear. Love is the opposite of fear, so if you love live music, come out and support it!

The set-list (at least for the early dates of the American leg of the tour and correct at time of writing) reads as follows:

'One More Time', 'Fabulously Absolute', 'Sunday Papers', 'Dave', 'Look Sharp!', 'Fool'. Solo ('So Low'), 'Real Men', 'Life On Mars', 'A Place In the Rain', 'Kings Of The City', 'Down To London', 'Blaze Of Glory', 'Sing You Sinners', 'Is She Really Going Out With Him?', 'It's Different For Girls', 'I'm The Man', with 'You Can't Get What You Want ('Till You Know What You Want'), and 'Steppin' Out' serving as encores.

So that's at least one completely new song receiving its premiere. This is, without doubt, something to be celebrated.

With four songs from his first album and three songs from his latest, this is another career covering collection. It says much for Jackson's quality levels, that there are so many other songs I would like to hear him perform as well. I doubt, however, that a four-plus hour concert is on the cards, somehow!

# The Author's Best of Joe Jackson

Jackson's reference to 'completely new material' surely implies that, at the time of writing, another studio album is in the works. Time will tell, and breaths are bated. Pending another fine collection of songs from the man I have compiled my own 'Best Of' playlist, taking one song from each album, avoiding the obvious choices; not out of mischief, just because there is so much more to Jackson than the occasional hit single suggests.

*Look Sharp!*: 'Fools In Love'

*I'm The Man*: 'The Band Wore Blue Shirts'

*Beat Crazy*: 'Someone Up There'

*Jumpin' Jive*: 'Jack, You're Dead'

*Night And Day*: 'A Slow Song'

*Mike's Murder*: 'Memphis'

*Body And Soul*: 'Not Here, Not Now'

*Big World*: 'Man In The Street'

*Will Power*: 'No Pasaran'

*Tucker...*: 'Vera'

*Blaze Of Glory*: 'Blaze Of Glory'

*Laughter & Lust*: 'Stranger Than Fiction'

*Night Music*: 'The Man Who Wrote 'Danny Boy''

*Heaven & Hell*: 'Fugue 2: Song Of Daedalus'

*Symphony No.1*: 'Fast Movement'

*Night And Day II*: 'Stranger Than You'

*Volume 4*: 'Still Alive'

*Rain*: 'Solo (So Low)'

*The Duke*: 'Isfahan'

*Fast Forward*: 'Kings Of The City'

*Fool*: 'Big Black Cloud'

# The Best Album Per Decade

Whilst I am, clearly, a huge fan of Jackson's eclectic output there are some albums which I have found harder to enjoy; step forward *Jumpin' Jive*, *Mike's Murder*, *Will Power*, *Tucker* and, strangely – no matter how hard I try – *Night And Day II*. But that's a low ratio over a five-decade, 21 album career, and having listened to these 'also-rans' a lot to write this book there is rewarding music in all of them. If you want to pick a 'best album per decade' which gives a sense of the scale of Jackson's abilities, I offer the following up for consideration;

1970s: *I'm The Man*: A master class of 'new wave', reggae, and pop writing.

1980s: *Body And Soul'*: Brilliant recorded sound, fantastic songs.

1990s: *Laugher And Lust*: Twelve pop-rock gems with a glistening sheen.

2000s: *Rain*: An impressive collection with stripped back instrumentation.

2010s: *Fool*: An almost back-to-basics album, on which seven out of the eight songs are superb.

2020s: ???... here's hoping!

# Joni Mitchell - *on track*

## every album, every song

Peter Kearns
Paperback
160 pages
35 colour photographs
978-1-78951-081-1
£14.99
$21.95

**Every album and
every song by this
legendary Canadian
singer-songwriter.**

In her long career, Canadian songstress Joni Mitchell has been hailed as everything from a 1960s folk icon to 20th century cultural figure, artistic iconoclast to musical heroine, extreme romantic confessor to both outspoken commentator and lyrical painter. Eschewing commercial considerations, she simply viewed her trajectory as that of any artist serious about the integrity of their work. But whatever musical position she took, she was always one step ahead of the game, making eclectic and innovative music.

Albums like *The Ladies Of The Canyon*, *Blue*, *Hejira* and *Mingus* helped define each era of the 1970s, as she moved from exquisitely pitched singer-songwriter material towards jazz. By the 1980s, her influence was really beginning to show via a host of imitators, many of them big names in their own right. He profound influence continues in popular music to this day.

This book revisits her studio albums in detail from 1968's *Song to a Seagull* to 2007's *Shine*, providing anecdote and insight into the recording sessions. It also includes an in-depth analysis both of her lyrics and the way her music developed stylistically over such a lengthy career, making this the most comprehensive book on this remarkable artist yet written.

# Elton John 1969 to 1979 - *on track*

## every album, every song

Peter Kearns
Paperback
144 pages
35 color photographs
978-1-78952-034-7
£14.99
USD 21.95

**Every track recorded by music legend Elton John during the 1970s, arguably his most creative and most commercial successful period.**

In 1970, Elton John, formerly Reginald Kenneth Dwight, stepped from the obscurity of suburban Pinner, Middlesex, England, into a pop culture reeling from post-Beatles fallout, to become one of the biggest-selling recording artists in the world. To date he has sold over 300 million records from a discography of 30 studio albums, four live albums, over 100 singles, and a multitude of compilations, soundtracks and collaborations. He is the recipient of six Grammys and ten Ivor Novello awards, was inducted into the Rock and Roll Hall of Fame in 1994, appointed a Commander of the Order of the British Empire in 1995 and knighted in 1998. In 2018 he embarked on what is intended to be his swansong world tour, *Farewell Yellow Brick Road*.

This book covers the period from Elton's earliest 1960s releases to his final 1970s album, *Victim of Love*. It is a critical overview of every track on the thirteen studio albums released in an era when Elton was at his most successful and that many fans consider to be the musical high-point of his career. Also included are the two live albums *17-11-70* and *Here and There*, and the trove of album-worthy B-sides that augmented the discography along the way.

# Peter Gabriel - *on track*
## every album, every song

Graeme Scarfe
Paperback
160 pages
40 colour photographs
978-178-952-138-2
£14.99
USD 21.95

**Every album recorded by this British pioneer of progressive music.**

If Genesis, according to British comedian and fan Al Murray 'were the progressive rock band who progressed', then Peter Gabriel as a solo artist would be the member that progressed the most. Who would have thought that listening to early Genesis would eventually take the listener to Senegal, Armenia, South Africa and beyond, via the artistic endeavours of their former vocalist?

This is a journey through Peter Gabriel's solo albums, his live recordings and soundtrack compositions. During his forty-year plus solo career, Gabriel has become a worldwide pop star via his early, self-titled albums and his seminal 1986 record

So. He has had hit singles throughout his career, including the bucolic 'Solsbury Hill' in 1977 and the poignant 'Don't Give Up'. He also helped pioneer video creativity with the song 'Sledgehammer'. In doing so, he has reached beyond his progressive rock origins to achieve a level of popularity and respect that other musicians from that genre could only dream about. You may have heard many of these songs before, but there's always something new to be found by digging in the dirt. This is the perfect guide to his music for new listeners and long-term fans alike.

What on earth is going on? In the words of the Burgermiester: 'I...will...find...out.'

## On Track series

Alan Parsons Project – Steve Swift 978-1-78952-154-2
Tori Amos – Lisa Torem 978-1-78952-142-9
Asia – Peter Braidis 978-1-78952-099-6
Badfinger – Robert Day-Webb 978-1-878952-176-4
Barclay James Harvest – Keith and Monica Domone 978-1-78952-067-5
The Beatles – Andrew Wild 978-1-78952-009-5
The Beatles Solo 1969-1980 – Andrew Wild 978-1-78952-030-9
Blue Oyster Cult – Jacob Holm-Lupo 978-1-78952-007-1
Blur – Matt Bishop – 978-178952-164-1
Marc Bolan and T.Rex – Peter Gallagher 978-1-78952-124-5
Kate Bush – Bill Thomas 978-1-78952-097-2
Camel – Hamish Kuzminski 978-1-78952-040-8
Caravan – Andy Boot 978-1-78952-127-6
Cardiacs – Eric Benac 978-1-78952-131-3
Eric Clapton Solo – Andrew Wild 978-1-78952-141-2
The Clash – Nick Assirati 978-1-78952-077-4
Crosby, Stills and Nash – Andrew Wild 978-1-78952-039-2
The Damned – Morgan Brown 978-1-78952-136-8
Deep Purple and Rainbow 1968-79 – Steve Pilkington 978-1-78952-002-6
Dire Straits – Andrew Wild 978-1-78952-044-6
The Doors – Tony Thompson 978-1-78952-137-5
Dream Theater – Jordan Blum 978-1-78952-050-7
Electric Light Orchestra – Barry Delve 978-1-78952-152-8
Elvis Costello and The Attractions – Georg Purvis 978-1-78952-129-0
Emerson Lake and Palmer – Mike Goode 978-1-78952-000-2
Fairport Convention – Kevan Furbank 978-1-78952-051-4
Peter Gabriel – Graeme Scarfe 978-1-78952-138-2
Genesis – Stuart MacFarlane 978-1-78952-005-7
Gentle Giant – Gary Steel 978-1-78952-058-3
Gong – Kevan Furbank 978-1-78952-082-8
Hall and Oates – Ian Abrahams 978-1-78952-167-2
Hawkwind – Duncan Harris 978-1-78952-052-1
Peter Hammill – Richard Rees Jones 978-1-78952-163-4
Roy Harper – Opher Goodwin 978-1-78952-130-6
Jimi Hendrix – Emma Stott 978-1-78952-175-7
The Hollies – Andrew Darlington 978-1-78952-159-7
Iron Maiden – Steve Pilkington 978-1-78952-061-3
Jefferson Airplane – Richard Butterworth 978-1-78952-143-6
Jethro Tull – Jordan Blum 978-1-78952-016-3
Elton John in the 1970s – Peter Kearns 978-1-78952-034-7
The Incredible String Band – Tim Moon 978-1-78952-107-8
Iron Maiden – Steve Pilkington 978-1-78952-061-3
Judas Priest – John Tucker 978-1-78952-018-7

Kansas – Kevin Cummings 978-1-78952-057-6
The Kinks – Martin Hutchinson 978-1-78952-172-6
Korn – Matt Karpe 978-1-78952-153-5
Led Zeppelin – Steve Pilkington 978-1-78952-151-1
Level 42 – Matt Philips 978-1-78952-102-3
Little Feat – 978-1-78952-168-9
Aimee Mann – Jez Rowden 978-1-78952-036-1
Joni Mitchell – Peter Kearns 978-1-78952-081-1
The Moody Blues – Geoffrey Feakes 978-1-78952-042-2
Motorhead – Duncan Harris 978-1-78952-173-3
Mike Oldfield – Ryan Yard 978-1-78952-060-6
Opeth – Jordan Blum 978-1-78-952-166-5
Tom Petty – Richard James 978-1-78952-128-3
Porcupine Tree – Nick Holmes 978-1-78952-144-3
Queen – Andrew Wild 978-1-78952-003-3
Radiohead – William Allen 978-1-78952-149-8
Renaissance – David Detmer 978-1-78952-062-0
The Rolling Stones 1963-80 – Steve Pilkington 978-1-78952-017-0
The Smiths and Morrissey – Tommy Gunnarsson 978-1-78952-140-5
Status Quo the Frantic Four Years – Richard James 978-1-78952-160-3
Steely Dan – Jez Rowden 978-1-78952-043-9
Steve Hackett – Geoffrey Feakes 978-1-78952-098-9
Thin Lizzy – Graeme Stroud 978-1-78952-064-4
Toto – Jacob Holm-Lupo 978-1-78952-019-4
U2 – Eoghan Lyng 978-1-78952-078-1
UFO – Richard James 978-1-78952-073-6
The Who – Geoffrey Feakes 978-1-78952-076-7
Roy Wood and the Move – James R Turner 978-1-78952-008-8
Van Der Graaf Generator – Dan Coffey 978-1-78952-031-6
Yes – Stephen Lambe 978-1-78952-001-9
Frank Zappa 1966 to 1979 – Eric Benac 978-1-78952-033-0
Warren Zevon – Peter Gallagher 978-1-78952-170-2
10CC – Peter Kearns 978-1-78952-054-5

## Decades Series
The Bee Gees in the 1960s – Andrew Mon Hughes et al 978-1-78952-148-1
The Bee Gees in the 1970s – Andrew Mon Hughes et al 978-1-78952-179-5
Black Sabbath in the 1970s – Chris Sutton 978-1-78952-171-9
Britpop – Peter Richard Adams and Matt Pooler 978-1-78952-169-6
Alice Cooper in the 1970s – Chris Sutton 978-1-78952-104-7
Curved Air in the 1970s – Laura Shenton 978-1-78952-069-9
Bob Dylan in the 1980s – Don Klees 978-1-78952-157-3
Fleetwood Mac in the 1970s – Andrew Wild 978-1-78952-105-4
Focus in the 1970s – Stephen Lambe 978-1-78952-079-8
Free and Bad Company in the 1970s – John Van der Kiste 978-1-78952-178-8

Also available from Sonicbond

Genesis in the 1970s – Bill Thomas 978178952-146-7
George Harrison in the 1970s – Eoghan Lyng 978-1-78952-174-0
Marillion in the 1980s – Nathaniel Webb 978-1-78952-065-1
Mott the Hoople and Ian Hunter in the 1970s – John Van der Kiste 978-1-78-952-162-7
Pink Floyd In The 1970s – Georg Purvis 978-1-78952-072-9
Tangerine Dream in the 1970s – Stephen Palmer 978-1-78952-161-0
The Sweet in the 1970s – Darren Johnson 978-1-78952-139-9
Uriah Heep in the 1970s – Steve Pilkington 978-1-78952-103-0
Yes in the 1980s – Stephen Lambe with David Watkinson 978-1-78952-125-2

## On Screen series
Carry On… – Stephen Lambe 978-1-78952-004-0
David Cronenberg – Patrick Chapman 978-1-78952-071-2
Doctor Who: The David Tennant Years – Jamie Hailstone 978-1-78952-066-8
James Bond – Andrew Wild – 978-1-78952-010-1
Monty Python – Steve Pilkington 978-1-78952-047-7
Seinfeld Seasons 1 to 5 – Stephen Lambe 978-1-78952-012-5

## Other Books
1967: A Year In Psychedelic Rock – Kevan Furbank 978-1-78952-155-9
1970: A Year In Rock – John Van der Kiste 978-1-78952-147-4
1973: The Golden Year of Progressive Rock 978-1-78952-165-8
Babysitting A Band On The Rocks – G.D. Praetorius 978-1-78952-106-1
Eric Clapton Sessions – Andrew Wild 978-1-78952-177-1
Derek Taylor: For Your Radioactive Children – Andrew Darlington 978-1-78952-038-5
The Golden Road: The Recording History of The Grateful Dead – John Kilbride 978-1-78952-156-6
Iggy and The Stooges On Stage 1967-1974 – Per Nilsen 978-1-78952-101-6
Jon Anderson and the Warriors – the road to Yes – David Watkinson 978-1-78952-059-0
Nu Metal: A Definitive Guide – Matt Karpe 978-1-78952-063-7
Tommy Bolin: In and Out of Deep Purple – Laura Shenton 978-1-78952-070-5
Maximum Darkness – Deke Leonard 978-1-78952-048-4
Maybe I Should've Stayed In Bed – Deke Leonard 978-1-78952-053-8
The Twang Dynasty – Deke Leonard 978-1-78952-049-1

*and many more to come!*

**Would you like to write for Sonicbond Publishing?**
We are mainly a music publisher, but we also occasionally
publish in other genres including film and television. At Sonicbond
Publishing we are always on the look-out for authors, particularly for
our two main series, On Track and Decades.

Mixing fact with in depth analysis, the On Track series examines
the entire recorded work of a particular musical artist or group. All
genres are considered from easy listening and jazz to 60s soul to 90s
pop, via rock and metal.

The Decades series singles out a particular decade in an artist or
group's history and focuses on that decade in more detail than may
be allowed in the On Track series.

While professional writing experience would, of course, be
an advantage, the most important qualification is to have real
enthusiasm and knowledge of your subject. First-time authors are
welcomed, but the ability to write well in English is essential.

Sonicbond Publishing has distribution throughout Europe and
North America, and all our books are also published in E-book form.
Authors will be paid a royalty based on sales of their book.
Further details about our books are available from
www.sonicbondpublishing.com. To contact us, complete the
contact form there or email info@sonicbondpublishing.co.uk